Practical Curiosity

PRACTICAL CURIOSITY

THE GUIDE TO LIFE, LOVE & TRAVEL

ALEX BERGER

Continue the conversation at
practicalcuriosity.com

Jacket art by Karolina Stankevičiūtė
Book design by Walton Mendelson

ISBN-13: 978-1-9763-0046-2
ISBN-10: 1-9763-0046-0

DEDICATION

To Dad, Mom and my brother David. You are the catalysts that set me upon this path, the mentors that have guided me, the muses which have inspired me, and the critical voices which have helped me to refine and improve. Your love and support paired with the paths you've charted through your own lives are the foundation upon which this book has come into being.

CONTENTS

ACKNOWLEDGMENTS

The ideas I introduce throughout the text are only possible due to the philosophers, academics, authors, podcasters and mentors who have shared their insights.

A further thank you is due to the friends who have shared their hearts and minds with me, the mentors who have helped shape my world view, my early-reviewers who offered invaluable feedback and my family who are an endless source of support, inspiration and encouragement.

PREFACE

Life is inherently complex. The life we live is also absolutely unique. From the moment we spring into existence to the moment our last breath slips free of our body, we are experiencing a world in a way which is fundamentally different than every other person who has come before us or who will follow in our footsteps.

This fascinates me and fuels my curiosity. After all, it is profoundly difficult to slip into another person's shoes and to explore their world view. As we gain access to the lessons they've learned from key individuals, parents and mentors, experiences which differ greatly from our own, we augment our understanding of our own lives.

I engage with business leaders, inspirational thinkers, and some of the world's greatest artists and explorers on a regular basis. Insatiable curiosity has been the key that has opened these doors. The success that I've found while chasing that curiosity has come from charting my way and viewing my experiences through a practical lens that constantly digests, evaluates and incorporates each new lesson learned or experience lived. This has led me to explore more than fifty different countries, cultures, and ways of thinking as well as helped me navigate through a diverse and rewarding business career.

This book is my attempt to take a wide cross-section of carefully crafted observations and share them with you. Over the following pages I run through thought exercises that have the potential to change how you understand and relate to the world. I explore life lessons and hard-earned realizations about what makes a person successful in life and business while dispelling commonly perpetuated myths. I will take you through an exploration of key relational observations which I find are re-occurring themes in people's lives. I draw upon my experiences as an expat, a sojourner, an exchange student, and a travel writer to share with you some of the most powerful lessons and observations that have come from a life shaped by extensive travels.

What you'll find in the following pages is a series of sections written in the voice best suited to deliver the message. At times I'll share personal stories and life lessons with you. In other sections I'll share general observations or deep dive and explore topics from a more traditionally academic perspective.

Through it all, my aspiration and commitment to you is to provide a cross-genre exploration of what it means to work towards being a well-rounded individual. This book will help you better understand and accept yourself. It is crafted to help you see the world through a different lens and to understand and garner life lessons learned while digging into oft-avoided topics and truths.

Practical Curiosity is an exploration of the mind of a generalist and an exercise in embracing voracious curiosity. It is about mastering self-doubt, overcoming fears, embracing personal development, and charting a course that doesn't treat success as a zero-sum game. I've incorporated concepts that are old, others that are in vogue, and some pulled from the leading edge of emerging scientific discovery. This book is a tool to help you digest, contextualize, and incorporate many of these concepts as they apply to lifestyle, business, relationships, and travel to achieve a more successful and fruitful life.

As you navigate the sections in this book, view each as a piece of a puzzle that gradually builds and fills in gaps. Use each new section to engage with and understand the next. Through it all, evaluate each observation and exercise not just as it relates to your own past experiences, but how it helps you move forward along your path to success.

Pick two friends or family members, one who is very similar to you and another who is very different. As you digest each concept put yourself in their shoes and explore how the section explains their world view and how the two of you interact.

As a final step ask yourself how you'd explain the key takeaways from that section to both friends. This process of summarizing, applying, and discussing will increase the value you draw from each section.

Thank you for entrusting me with your time, your curiosity and your open mind.

Practical Curiosity

THOUGHT EXERCISES

I HAVE FOUND that the following thought experiments are wonderful tools that have played a pivotal role in shaping how I perceive and interact with the world. The goal of each of these exercises is twofold. First, they help to understand and explain people, behaviors and their decision-making. Second, they help me to explain and become comfortable with my own needs.

Personal development and self-awareness often require a mental framework which you can use to understand and test certain assumptions. I find it's also the best way to explore my relationship with cultural norms or issues I would otherwise avoid completely.

To get the most out of these exercises, I suggest working through them multiple times. It's also best if you get comfortable sitting or lying down in a place that is quiet without disturbances or distractions to ensure you have time to digest and reflect. Each exercise will take you no more than five to ten minutes.

The Dark Room and the Door

The Exercise

The dark room and the door thought experiment is designed to help you understand your personal balance between the known vs. the unknown and your tolerance for comfort vs. discomfort. Different areas of our lives by necessity require different behaviors, but this is a great way to explore and discuss what you want from life and where you are most fulfilled. It's also a tool for deciding if you're happy with where you are or if you should make some changes.

To start, picture that you come into existence alone, into an utterly unchanging environment. You are tabula rasa, a blank slate, in an environment that is completely static and without variation. There is only the temperature as it is—no hot, no cold, no fluctuations. There is no stimulation and no contrast. Only existence. You just are. In this state, you're neither happy nor unhappy. You exist.

Now, consider two alternate series of events. In one, nothing changes. In the other, a doorway suddenly appears and offers the prospect of exiting the space and entering the outside world. Depending on your level of curiosity, you may choose to open the doorway and pass into a world of contrasts and diverse experiences. For this exercise, explore your emotional response as you visualize moving further from the doorway and deeper into a wider array of experiences and uncertainty.

In that world the static state of being without context is replaced by things like love, vibrant flavors, discovery, knowledge, pleasure, and sensations of hot and cold. Each of these is profoundly attractive, right? But, there's a catch. With them also comes the other side of each—war, ugly colors, loss, heartache, and pain.

Which individual is happier? The one that never left the room or the individual who threw the door open and went running through? In truth, if the pure measure is happiness or contentment then the answer is the first individual—the one that stayed in the room. That individual will be, almost without fail, much more content or 'happier' than the other. But, for the individual driven and stimulated by curiosity, the overall experience they enjoy as they move further into the world will be richer. True, unlike the individual who remained in the room, they will experience pain, heartbreak and suffering, cold rainy days, sickness, discomfort and much more. But with it, they gain access and insight to an ever-growing tapestry of experiences. How far from the doorway are you comfortable wandering?

This is the same concept that periodically pops up in books and movies. In the Matrix it was the red pill/blue pill; live in an artificial world or face the realities of an apocalyptic and grim real world. In other novels, it's the story of the character who grows up in a small town and then goes on to explore the wide world enriched by incredible experiences. It's relevant in other areas of our lives as well. For example, the concept of no sex until marriage has evolved to be based heavily around this type of narrative. After all, if the entire frame of reference you're basing your sexual experience on is tied exclusively to one individual then you're more likely to be content in that state, regardless of if it's good or bad. Does it work? It often depends—are you the first type or second type of individual?

The challenge comes when the complexities of our social networks provide that 'doorway' perspective. Suddenly, you're faced with the knowledge that there are other options and that perhaps what you take to be good is radically worse than what is potentially out there. But, at the same time, the likelihood remains that as you add to your experiences, your expectations change. You become harder to satisfy, have a wider list of needs and expectations and for every significantly better partner that you discover, you will likely find several that come up short.

For the individual who likes as little diversity in their diet as possible, who sticks to a set routine, a close group of friends and their hometown—they've embraced the static comfort of the dark room. It's also likely very true, though not popular to say, that these individuals are happier.

I am a profoundly curious person in most aspects of my life. While through this exercise I've come to accept that the cost of that curiosity is being less content with life as it is, I am profoundly grateful that I have chosen to feed my curiosity and to experience the full depth, breadth, and richness of life.

For me personally, embracing unabashedly the curiosity that drives those experiences and brings that contrast in life allows me to explore a spectrum of sensations, questions, and emotions that adds a richness, meaning, and level of stimulation to my life that

I treasure. This more than offsets the frustrations or discomfort that also periodically arise.

Ultimately, neither is wrong. But, understanding the difference in our needs, where we place and draw value, and what drives us is essential for a healthy understanding of ourselves and those around us.

The Ant & The Universe

When I was a child, my Dad had me sit down and walked me through an exercise. It's one I've modified since that time and used to explore my place in the Universe, to come to terms with the existence of things we lack words or the ability to visualize, and to hone my ability to explore the complexities of the world around me and the people in it. Depending on the way your mind works and your ability to visualize mentally, you may have to explore variations of this technique.

The Exercise

Picture the front right foot of an ant. Take a moment to explore the structure of the foot and work to fill in as much detail or richness as you can in your mental image. It's not essential that you hold the whole image in your mind—more that you run your mental fingers across each aspect, working to picture it and keeping its presence in the back of your mind.

Now, step back incrementally, not unlike a camera zooming out. Picture how that right foot connects to the leg joints and the rest of the ant's right leg.

Step back again, this time visualizing the ant as a

whole, filling your mind's eye with the image of the
ant as it exists.

Step back. Consider the space immediately around
the ant—the tunnel immediately surrounding it, the
other ants in its immediate proximity.

Step back. Consider the ant colony as a whole.
Pausing to let your mind wander through the complexity of the social hierarchy, the simultaneous
dance as thousands of ants go about their business
and respond to a large range of different experiences,
stimuli, and in numerous different roles. Consider
the ants trapped by a cave in, the ant larva hatching,
the queen ... and move beyond just the ants and their
tunnels. Consider the worms in the soil. The com-
position of that soil. The smell in the air. The ant was
your focal point, but your focus is now on embracing
and mentally exploring every aspect big and small in
the area you're visualizing.

Step back. Consider the patch of ground three feet
in every direction surrounding the ant hill. Is it
stripped barren, is it full of life? Why? How?

Step back. Consider the small meadow that the
ant hill sits in. Leave behind the ants themselves and
work to understand the leaves, the complexity of the
plants, the trees, the animals that live there and their
dynamics.

Step back. Consider the small forest that the
meadow sits within.

Step back. Consider. Step back. Consider. Each
time taking an incremental step. From the forest to
the national park. From the national park to the nearby city. Then the region. Then the state. Then the
country. Then the continent.

Step back.

Eventually, I want you to find yourself floating above the earth. Consider the clouds, the weather, the changing seasons. Consider not only the cities but the people in the cities and the passing of time. Through it all, pause and remember that even now, as impossibly complex as it is to track and understand that view of people and cities and nations, that beneath it all, is another layer, all the way down to that lone ant and a layer that exists beneath it all.

Step back. Now to the Moon as it circles the Earth.

Step back. Now to the Moon and Earth circling the Sun.

Step back. Take in the solar system and all its complexities and moving parts and reflect on how they include everything all the way back down to that one lone ant.

Step back. Visualize the 500+ solar systems that sit in our Galaxy.

Step back. Consider that our lone Galaxy with all of its moving pieces is one of more than 100 billion galaxies in the Universe.

But, now a problem arises. For most people, you'll hit an impasse. For others, you'll be able to take a few more steps back—exploring multiverse theory or concepts like white holes. But ultimately, you'll reach a threshold where we lack the knowledge, words, and way of visualizing what comes next.

As you work through this thought exercise, the areas you focus on, the elements you seek to understand, and your level of comfort with the sheer scope and scale evolves over time.

So, Why Is This Interesting?

We inherently see the world through our own eyes. Eyes that look outward and are shaped by our experiences, by our priorities, and by our immediate needs. I love this exercise because it fundamentally puts me in a different mindset and challenges me to explore and make myself aware of my surroundings and the profound complexity of what's otherwise invisible.

On the one hand, it reminds me of how incredible my impact is on those near me. In one afternoon with a backhoe, I have the power to wipe out, reshape, and transform that entire forest meadow. Over time, with the help of a few others, I can create a dam fundamentally re-shaping the path of entire rivers and ecosystems. In doing so, my impact is staggeringly profound and will echo like ripples in a pond for much longer than I would otherwise imagine.

On the other hand, it reminds me of how minuscule and fleeting my time here is. It is a powerful reminder that despite my ability to change the world around me, I am still every bit as small as that ant. That despite the importance of my daily life, I'm just one of many in an astoundingly large and complex universe.

It also helps me understand just how different the environment, life, culture, and existence is for other people. It allows me to visualize elements of my daily life sitting at a desk in the heart of Copenhagen, while simultaneously attempting to at least expose myself to a crude mental rendering of how that may compare to your experience as you sit reading this text. Or to that of a young child raised in a remote village in rural China.

With that understanding in hand, it also provides me with a strong sense of meaning. I feel this exercise leaves me with a much richer understanding of life and a feeling of significance. True, it makes me feel small—especially when I try and add the dimension of time to it. But, it also helps me understand that my actions do have an impact and have the potential to resonate, quite literally changing the world around me.

Imagining the Unimaginable

In completing this exercise, you've run through the evolution of human awareness and explored our rapidly evolving understanding of what's around us. Step back through time 300 years and consider what they understood of the Universe. Then back in time 2,000 years. 5,000 years?

What we take for granted and can understand at a basic level, simple things like the knowledge that existence is not confined to the surface of the earth or that our earth circles the sun, were inaccessible for our ancestors. And yet, here we stand today with those concepts not only accessible but completely mundane and boring.

Now place yourself in the shoes of that ancestor. Consider, without shame, guilt, condescension or frustration that we no doubt are equally ignorant of what might be out there. As astronomically large as the jump from an ant to a planet may be or a planet to a Universe may be—the next step, what comes af-

ter a universe may be equally surmountable once we
have the tools to understand it.

But, don't stop there. Now, take your mental image of the Universe—it probably looks in your
mind's eye a bit like a galaxy, all spots of light, spiral-
ing around a central source point—and consider
what's beyond the edge of that universe.

Interestingly, we have the tools and context now
to visualize the Universe itself, but the image of what
is beyond is something that for most of us can only
be imagined in two ways. We are taught to "see"
black and to think of that "space" beyond the Universe as void. But, consider. Can you actually picture
void in your mind's eye? Keeping in mind that void
here is the concept of not just emptiness, but actually
of the absence of everything.

Somehow, as a species, we've developed the language to describe a phenomenon that is so far outside how our brains work that it is impossible to
visualize or to even fully conceptually understand its
existence. Even picturing endless blackness is inaccurate as void is the absence of all. It's a fascinating
quandary because simultaneously you're picturing and
considering what must "exist," but which at the same
time cannot.

Even further, think of it a bit like a sealed room
without oxygen. While not a true void that's perhaps
the easiest and closest direct comparison. Then consider what happens when air is introduced. Consider
how it disperses and floods to fill the space, consuming and replacing the void. But, now consider that in
the context of our Universe, there is no sealed room—
the two are reversed. That, eventually, no matter how

far you scale up—eventually there should be a ring of void circling the universe (or collection of universes) that simply is. And consider, if that void is what is beyond "here," then how is it that it is simultaneously void—something that is nothing—and at the same time co-exists with existence.

If this all makes your head hurt, you're not alone. But, it's a unique opportunity to explore a key aspect of how our brains work and who we are. It's also a very different way of exploring the core question at the root of religion. The Abrahamic faiths have God creating the Universe. Some scientific circles have the big bang as a spark that ignites the Universe. While both provide a comfortable starting point, what both neglect is a thought exercise on how to explore the presence of void.

Where I find this to be particularly useful, above and beyond exploring concepts of religion or existence, is in helping me to cope with the existence of much more lightweight concepts. It provides a way of relating to, exploring and understanding, what it would be like to be the first person to experience zero gravity. Or an individual who has never heard, or seen, or encountered snow before and then suddenly discovers it on their own.

While it's impossible to imagine some of the new experiences, or creations, or possibilities likely to evolve in our lifetime, this exercise gives us a framework for preparing for those discoveries and for being open to and embracing them. How does one know and imagine the unknowable? By creating comfort with and befriending the essence of how we relate to and accept that unknown when it arrives.

This exercise is ultimately about finding comfort with the uncomfortable. About learning to embrace a perspective and about extending our awareness beyond the confines of our own inner self.

The Toilet Paper Exercise

I want you to take a moment to reflect on the many times you emptied your bowels—yes, we've gone from discussing the vastness of the Universe to talking about the last time you pooped. As part of a graphic stroll down memory lane, consider how you cleansed yourself afterward. It's an essential part of your daily routine, one that you've likely partaken in, at least once a day, for nearly every day of your life. You should, at a basic level, also consider yourself a relative expert at it.

Now, consider your existing wiping method.

Ask yourself—how would you do it if you weren't going to use your normal method?

If you're like most people, you probably have some difficulty envisioning alternatives. The majority of us assume that there's more or less only one way to wipe our butt—the way our parents taught us.

But, for paper-wielding bum cleansers, there are actually two distinct approaches: those who fold and those who scrunch. The folder takes several carefully chosen tiles of tissue, folds them over for durability and then wipes. You know that super cheap toilet paper that never seems to work well? For the folder, it's because that cheap paper has minimal texture, which, is the real reason more expensive toilet paper comes with a series of printed patterns and textures.

That quilted pattern and adorable animal print? It's not an art piece to fancy up toilet paper. It's a source of added texture and grip like the tread on your car tires.

Now, enter the scruncher. Those who scrunch will find the idea of folding as alien as scrunching is to the average folder. Unlike the folder, the scruncher takes a small ball of toilet paper and then uses that ball. While the scruncher probably needs more than the standard two squares, the scrunching method itself solves the paper tread issue folders risk encountering. In scrunching, the scruncher has created maximum texture.

Perhaps you're aware of the difference. Most people aren't. It wasn't until I was 27 and stumbled on a random Reddit article that I had my world shattered.

Now, why the hell is this here? Because, for most of us, it's the perfect illustration of how something that is fundamental to our daily lives, that we consider ourselves relative experts in, and that we generally assume is only done one way—can be completely wrong.

Before reading about the scruncher/folder divide, I assumed that everyone around me would, of course, fold, as that was the only way to do it and the only option. Wrong. And more significantly, if something as simple and straight forward as that can be off, which of my other assumptions are also subject to re-assessment?

The truth is that the scruncher/folder divide is just the tip of the iceberg. In truth, as a civilization, we have a dozen ways of cleansing. From bum guns to buckets and bidets, automatic toilets, flushing toilets, squat toilets, hand flushing toilets and everything else in-between.

You also have the sitting-wipe vs. standing-wipe divide or in what most women will find shocking the front to back vs. back to front wipe divide.

Now, my challenge to you—take what we've run through in this section and consider just how that might be applied to other aspects of your life. This has the potential to be anything from how, when and where you eat your breakfast, to your perception of race or other religions. You can use it to better understand the people around you, or if you're in an entrepreneurial mode, to better understand and identify powerful opportunities that present themselves as a direct result of identifying these blind differences.

The Divine Phytoplankton Experiment

Without diving into theology in any great depth, there has always been one element that has nagged at me. That is, ultimately, the interplay between monotheistic religion, polytheistic religion, religion in general, and science in general. Creation myths vary widely but ultimately struggle with the essential question of where did existence come from and what created it.

While we often think of the Greek gods like Zeus, Poseidon, etc. as the originators of their universe and the ultimate supreme beings, they're relatively late in the creation myth. The Greek gods of Olympus are little more than children of children who ultimately give birth to humanity as their own progeny.

The Abrahamic faiths (Judaism, Christianity, and Islam), take a somewhat different approach with a supreme divine authority responsible for the creation and origin myth. Yet, that God still cedes some power to prophets, angels, or in the case of Jesus, various incarnations or reinventions of its divine self.

In the pursuit of answering that most obnoxious of questions, who are we and where did the Universe come from? I ran into a quandary that fascinated me. The Christians adhere to a narrative that God always existed and at some point decided to create the Universe. The Greeks followed a fairly similar path, though, in place of one God, numerous divine beings are involved with varying degrees of power and presence. Many of which are heavily tied to the elements and core behaviors. Meanwhile, the most widely accepted concept scientifically is that of the big bang, or potentially the big bounce.

None of these manages to do a good job of explaining what created the creator or sparked the point of creation. The Christian has an eternal God that has and will always exist. The Greek has Chaos which gave birth to the Earth. Modern science either cites insufficient information or the possibility that things are either cyclical or that there is a genuine starting point, but it is one that merely is and always has been. Of course, each individual faith has its own take and weights each deity or deities differently, but ultimately most boil down to the same similar challenges.

Which is where phytoplankton entered the equation as a tool for understanding perception and offered a lens for accepting that we have insufficient knowledge and that moving forward that knowledge is likely to expand to encompass new things far outside our existing reach. Growing up in Christian America, the concept of an omnipresent, absolute, omnipotent God is a cornerstone of the generally accepted worldview. But, agreement on how powerful God is, how omnipotent, and how involved in the day-to-day is a source of endless debate and contention.

So, the questions become: What's the best way to adapt to this new information as we discover it? How do I best come to understand what godly powers are? And then, how do I create a mental framework for relating to the Universe that does not require profound cognitive dissonance to be successful? And what exactly does it mean to be a god anyway?

To do this, I made a casual mental list of key things we commonly attribute to god or gods. The list included the basics, things like the ability to create the world, to modify landscapes at a profound scale, to seemingly give and create or modify life, and either immortality or extended mortality so far beyond the confines of what is within our perception that it seems to be immortality.

Then, I draw on the Ant Thought Experiment, which I've outlined previously, and decide to go even smaller. While an ant's world is interesting, it's still within a timeframe and scope that is marginally similar to ours as humans. Which eventually led me to settle on phytoplankton. To refresh, phytoplankton are so tiny they're essentially invisible to the naked human eye unless a massive bloom is occurring.

Their lifespan is brief, often only days, but they are also incredibly numerous and vary widely in type.

To begin with, put yourself in a phytoplankton's metaphorical shoes. You're a relatively simple organism, floating in what seems like an endless world. You're surrounded by trillions of your companions and your multi-cellular intelligence is effective for substance and reproduction, but you aren't likely to spout Shakespeare or discuss the origin of ethics anytime soon.

But, for the sake of this exercise, then consider what twenty-first century humans consider god-like traits and do it from your phytoplankton's perspective. As, hopefully, we can all agree that humans are not divine and are quite far from being gods themselves, let's consider our own species as it might be perceived by our wide-eyed phytoplankton.

Humans have the ability to re-shape the world. We've drained seas, created lakes the size of seas, leveled mountains and can manipulate the landscape of the earth on a profoundly impactful level. We're also able to create light and energy. It would even be possible to take our phytoplankton, create an artificial habitat for it by re-combining basic elements to create water, specific types of soil, and oxygen and then transport that artificial habitat into space. We're also rapidly gaining the ability to edit, recombine and modify genes and genetic markers in a way that bears a striking similarity to creating life.

But, beyond the ability to craft and modify the world at large, also consider physical size. Our titanic size in comparison to the phytoplankton would be daunting, and our physical strength so profoundly powerful that a flick of a finger would obliterate our hapless phytoplankton. To the phytoplankton's perspective where lives are lived in a day, perhaps two— our life spans as humans are beyond perception. Consider, to our phytoplankton with its 48-hour lifespan, how minutes would seem like days and then consider that over the duration of a 100-year human life span more than 52,594,920 minutes would pass.

Last, consider that where our phytoplankton is relegated to a brief period of experience and whatever genetic memory might be hard-wired into its genetic code, how the sum of human knowledge must seem. Begin by considering the level of knowledge you'll have accrued by your eightieth birthday. Then, consider how that is supplemented through the internet, books, word of mouth, language and everything in between. As a species, and you as a member of that species, have at your fingertips visual records of virtually all parts of the earth, combined with extensive historical and predictive data. To the limited perspective of our bright-eyed phytoplankton, you are, in effect, omnipotent.

So, what's the takeaway here? We know we're not gods. In fact, we know that there is a universe that surrounds us that we do not understand. Ultimately, we find ourselves in a world where we are that wide-eyed phytoplankton. To this end, the traits that we have historically attributed to the divine rapidly become less daunting and overwhelming.

In a Universe full of billions of galaxies filled with billions upon billions of solar systems, each home to billions of planets, it's not inconceivable that there might be entities, experiences, or occurrences so alien and gigantic in nature that they take on divine attributes. Ultimately, our Universe may serve as a home to creatures as different from us as we are from phytoplankton. While for some this may become a question of divinity or theism, I encourage you to instead focus on it as a way of framing, understanding and familiarizing yourself with the discomfort of the unknown.

In the end, what seems unknowable, what we lack the vocabulary for, and what is of such significant scope that it leaves us awed and humbled, may, in reality, be surprisingly simple. Once, that is, we change our perspective and analyze the situation through new and rapidly emerging contexts. Often how we look at something is every bit as important as what we're looking at.

LIFE LESSONS AND
LIFESTYLE REVELATIONS

As we chart our path through life we are often faced with three options. We can experiment blindly and learn from the results. We can experiment and observe, watching those in immediate proximity to us as they experiment alongside us and seek to incorporate their revelations. Or we can seek out wisdom from mentors and innovators, experiment and blend that with our observations.

In life, we all have those moments where we burn our fingers, despite the warnings and having just watched someone else make the same mistake. But, I find life is significantly more rewarding when we aspire to keep these unnecessarily, painful, first-hand life lessons to a minimum.

This book and the subsections in this chapter are a mixture of knowledge drawn from all three types of experimentation but with a heavy focus on essential insights into what it means to live life fully and successfully while furthering one's career drawn directly from incredible mentors. For those familiar with Sun Tzu's *The Art of War*, you'll recognize that sometimes the most beautiful life lessons are hidden in plain sight, often surfaced by seemingly obvious observations and guidance.

In this chapter, I aspire to walk the line between drawing your attention to things you may already know but will benefit from revisiting, alongside other deeper observations and life lessons that hopefully help you avoid hard-learned lessons and painful mistakes. The ultimate advantage should be your ability to live and understand your daily and professional life through a fresh lens in a healthy and more productive way. If, along the way, I can provide food for thought from well outside your regular worldview?

All the better.

Success and the Tribulations of a Generalist

Since I was a child, I've looked up to and aspired to the ideal of a Renaissance man or polymath, which is to say an individual that aspires toward many different traits and areas of expertise; who seeks to develop competence, if not mastery, in all.

As a child growing up one of the role models that always inspired me was the fictional starship captain Jean-Luc Picard. I also draw from my parents, both of whom are wonderfully erudite, down to earth, and gifted generalists.

At the core of each of these individuals, philosophies and characters are a fundamental driving curiosity which casts a wide net and, while all fundamentally interconnected, dilutes the attention an individual can dedicate to any one area. This dilution tends to trigger a lot of confusion, and I think also leads to a mischaracterization of different types of generalists. Distilled down to its simplest form I've come to see it as two types: The bold generalist vs. the timid generalist. The bold generalist has a voracious curiosity and devours new and diverse knowledge in contrast to the timid generalist, who is someone who operates in a state of paralyzed fear and limited curiosity resulting in bland mediocrity and a tendency to self-sabotage before moving on.

Unfortunately, we live in a world that not only fails to make the distinction between bold and timid generalists but also views and speaks to generalists in general with a level of disdain. In recent years as the focus in education and business has pivoted to Science, Technology, Engineering and Math (STEM), the traditional domain of the generalist, the humanities, has suffered significantly.

A cultural narrative has evolved that defines value, career worth, and success in terms of near absolutes tailored heavily towards specialization. As individuals we're ushered towards picking our area, specializing and becoming the very best. Part and parcel of that, also inherently includes defining our vision of success and self-worth from that ability to specialize, to have a committed plan over an extended period of time which moves us along a carefully calculated course.

The benefits to this are clear. It's more easily

digestible and we all have friends or individuals we look up to and/or evaluate ourselves against who have known since they were six that they were destined to become a thoracic surgeon or molecular biologist specializing in cell expression.

Often, these individuals invest significant time and effort in the process of attaining those goals, and the progression is easy to track and quantify. Which is not, of course, to say this is only the case in STEM fields. It applies equally to the prima ballerina or world's premier expert in Etruscan sculpture. For many of these individuals, a singular driving purpose is an essential fuel that lights the spark of their soul and ignites their passion.

The bold generalist, on the other hand, faces a frustrating quandary and constant crisis of self-worth. The old adage 'Jack of all trades, master of none' laced with its hints of mild disdain embodies the challenge these individuals face, myself included. The single-minded dedication required for absolute mastery or systemic and formulaic completion of tasks to attain recognition/pay come with fundamental and often unavoidable opportunity costs that contrast with the burning curiosity that perpetually tugs me and my interests in a multitude of directions. It is this diversity of interests, passions, topics, and knowledge which—almost counterintuitively—is the end goal for me. The driving desire to have the most complete and in-depth knowledge possible across all of the available topics helps me better understand each topic more completely, within context.

In this way, I suppose I *am* a specialist, just not the

"right kind" of specialist. I've just chosen to replace learning the periodic table, or every muscle in the body, with similar ingredients and strands of knowledge. The value that I derive from this is the ability to make connections and to contextualize the knowledge I encounter in a more three-dimensional and nonlinear context.

Unfortunately, by its very nature, that context and process does not compute directly to a more formulaic structure or dedicated advancement within a pre-established system of protocols. By this, I in no way mean one approach is superior to the other. Quite the opposite, the two are inherently complementary. The very foundation I operate upon is provided for by specialists and requires their focused and dedicated deep dive into their topic of expertise.

But by that same stroke, I hope that in sharing this, I help those of you reading and reflecting who may find yourselves in similar positions, that the value and level of my success and accomplishments are not diminished by not conforming to a specialist's structure. Similar to the fibers in a muscle, if you take one, isolate it, and evaluate it purely on its own merit—it seems weak, feeble, limited and incomplete. Which, of course, is true. It's only when you evaluate that fiber as part of a band of fibers, operating as part of an integrated muscular system that you draw upon and understand the full value and accomplishment of that individual fiber.

All of this leads to that inevitable gut check—that moment where you have to ask yourself, at this point in life am I successful? It's a question that has terrified me and I've struggled with it since my mid-teens. I have not become the Jacques Cousteau of my generation, the Neil Armstrong, or Sergey Brin. But here's the thing, not only is that perfectly ok, I wouldn't have it any other way.

Thus far I've crafted a life that has rewarded and fed my voracious curiosity while enabling my passions as a bold generalist. That's not to say it hasn't brought with it career success and that I don't have a level of craftsmanship and perfectionism to my work and pursuits. It just means that the rubric I grade myself against is fundamentally different than what our cultural narrative throughout western society aggressively pushes for. Ultimately it means coming to terms with the nagging doubt of, "Sure, I've accomplished things, but what could I accomplish if I ever truly focused my abilities on one thing?"

It sounds like a simple and silly thing and yet at the same time I know that it constantly gives friends endless pain and self-doubt. Sadly, I also suspect that the related emotional conflict has also led several friends to commit suicide. There is a delicate and difficult balance to strike when you harbor the drive to be a specialist, but have it unleashed and dispersed across a wide net of interests. The reward itself is the knowledge, the cost is a schism in understanding between the people and cultural messages around you and what your gut tells you to be true. This creates a powerful struggle as we work to redefine the terms by which we track and evaluate our personal success, priorities, and goals.

Interestingly you see some of this at work within elements of the silicon valley technorati. These individuals who have excelled relatively early in life and who were, initially, either heavily oriented towards a specialist approach or generalists who forced themselves to conform for the sake of operating within the system laid out for them. Only now, with the success criteria satisfied—millions made, companies built and sold, and "success" defined—these same individuals are now drifting, struggling, and lost as they work diligently to retool themselves and their minds. From meditation to a heavy push towards stoicism, most have pivoted towards chasing that Renaissance man ideal through a diversified approach of introspection, curiosity, and reflection.

To this end, I've come to utterly disdain the well-meaning but deeply damaging question we pose to children: "What do you want to be when you grow up?" For years I worried when I changed degrees or left a wonderful job opportunity behind, that I was fundamentally sabotaging and sacrificing my future. That I was betraying the people who believed in me and that I was throwing away years of work. Dad always told me, "Buy yourself out of the system." I've finally come to accept that the meaning there is much more than merely the monetary logistics. It's the intellectual and emotional capital to define success on my own terms and to accomplish and achieve the lifestyle and life-experience *I* want.

The reality is that I am successful, that I am happy, and that I am advancing and evolving the essence of who I am. That I am refining my ethos constantly, shaping and re-crafting who I am and what I value to better align with my goals while taking care to nurture and understand the pathos of how I engage with those around me and as importantly with myself. All the while, my foundation remains rooted in a logos that is the engine which drives my burning curiosity.

So, to those of you reading this book, especially those still studying and feeling deeply uncertain about the future, my message is simple: It's ok. Dedicate yourself to being good at what you do, chase your passion, do the grunt work where necessary, but don't feel as though you're locked in, treading water, or not accomplishing things just because your interests are varied.

So often we get the career advice, "find your passion... find your true calling... chase your dream." For a subset of us, it's absolute horseshit. There is no one passion. There is no one pure dream and in many cases to realize whatever we would latch onto to fill that role would ultimately crush the joy turning it into lifeless dust. If your true calling and passion is the pursuit of knowledge, curiosity, and the constant exploration of a wealth of topics and areas, then that's wonderful. It's a successful pursuit.

Paths to Success

The road to success is often introduced as a series of tangible and replicable steps. While this may work in some cases, far too often those steps are over simplified or missing key context. I've found that far more valuable than these types of advice are more structural, big picture, pieces of advice that require we refocus, change, or develop essential behaviors. These are more valuable as they deliver a skill set that creates opportunities and paths to success which are aligned to our personality, needs, industry and definition of success.

Embrace Passions

Our lives are full of passions. The big challenge, however, is that these passions often don't feel overt, concrete, or like the type of easily defined "passion," we expect. Ask people who have accomplished a lot what their passions are, and you'll get a mixture of answers. Many will give you a rehearsed elevator pitch born out of necessity due to the regular nature of the question. Others will shrug and have trouble answering. I know that I have a number of passions and I am perpetually active with projects, ideas, and engagements.

Yet, over the last decade, I have often struggled with this question—feeling as though I lack a defining passion. The reality is that embracing opportunities, pushing ourselves to say yes to new challenges, and exploring what stimulates us is all that is necessary for a life full of passion. These may be hard to explain or recount—but so is what you did yesterday.

Why? For the same reason. When we live lives immersed in our passions, they become part of who we are, seemingly mundane and rapidly integrated into our everyday experience. It is only with outside eyes that the reality is revealed.

Choose the Right People

Success is heavily influenced by the people you surround yourself with. Seek out the people. They are out there but perhaps not where you're looking. I've known some truly brilliant people who surrounded themselves with the uninspired, unintelligent, or those who lacked the emotional maturity to take action or take ownership for their own lives and identities.

There's an old saying that the path to wisdom is ensuring that you're always the least intelligent person in the room. If you want to succeed and if you want to push yourself to become a richer and more robust person, choose who you surround yourself with carefully.

Don't just look at how intelligent, or successful the people around you are. Look at what type of people they are. You will mirror them—and if they lack empathy, humanity, or integrity, they have every bit the negative impact on who you are and who you become as people who are uninspired or unmotivated. Finding the people you want to surround yourself with is no easy task. It often requires revisiting our daily routine, where we go, what we are involved with, and the people we meet as a result.

Chase Stimulation

I am a stimulation junkie. I don't mean this in the sense of drugs—something I've always avoided completely as I view my mind as something not to be toyed with idly. I mean it in the sense that with travel as a passion and as someone who is extremely curious, I find myself perpetually seeking new experiences and sources of stimulation.

From flavorful foods to new cultures, to history, to

architecture, or even social interactions—I am restless. This is something I love about myself and something that I constantly seek to nurture. However, it is also something that I've recently realized I have to be aware of.

Why? Because while it opens up doors and is part of what gives me the energy to pursue and explore the things I do, it can also distract me from taking a deeper or more prolonged dive into experiences. In short, the pursuit of new stimuli is deeply important, rewarding, and healthy but must be tempered by a connection to follow through and a head-nod to practical factors and considerations.

It's all well and good to chase the next adventure with a new dragon to find and slay. But, from time to time, we must also pause and make sure we take the time to actually complete that quest, to slay the dragon, and then to properly relish the adventure we've just undertaken.

Document Success

Another key area I'm working on is learning to celebrate, document, and be open about my achievements. I often think about being a child and looking forward to my birthday or holiday gifts. I would dream for months about some item, toy, or prize. Then, upon getting it, I'd enjoy it for a stretch before my attentions oh-so-often moved on to the next item or experience to pursue. I find that successes are a bit like this. I'm hard wired to constantly perform. To achieve new things and to focus on the next challenge. It is a formula that keeps me busy and has pushed me to accomplish a lot at an early age.

Still, one thing I'm horrible about is actually documenting and acknowledging these accomplishments. True, I'll share them with friends or family, and I am undoubtedly incredibly proud of them when they occur. But, they fade from sight and from mind quickly. This can be an issue when I hit unexpected delays or am reflecting on life and my accomplishments. During these periods I tend to be overly hard on myself failing to acknowledge or at times even remember many of the relevant accomplishments I have achieved. This overachiever dilemma is a challenging one. In no small part because documenting and cataloging accomplishments takes time and energy that seems better spent doing something.

At the same time, failure to do so leaves us unbalanced and warps our perspective. I've seen numerous friends and colleagues who were prolific overachievers and had accomplished great things fall victim to crippling (or sometimes lethal) self-doubt. While I've never felt that far out of balance, a cornerstone of success is being attuned to what you are doing, what you have done, and what you are capable of. It is also just flat out healthy to celebrate and document when a new milestone is achieved.

Learn to Accept Praise

As part of learning to celebrate achievements a key skill to develop is learning how to accept praise. Frankly, I suck at it. It's complex, it is uncomfortable, and it is awkward. It is also essential. Learn how to be gracious. Learn how to be humble. But also learn how to accept praise and accolades. Also, realize and accept that praise is not always all about you.

The person that benefits most or feels the greatest reward from praise may be someone else entirely. Just as we listen to a loved one's tired old story time and time again because we acknowledge that the telling gives them pleasure—be open to and accept that accolades and praise are just as often about those around you and those who care about you. Embrace it and see it as an opportunity to share a small gift with them.

Be Multidisciplinary

Be multidisciplinary if you want to understand any concept and be successful. In college, it always baffled me that economics students learned so little history, sociology, or anthropology. The result was disastrous and led to grossly unbalanced economists with massive holes in their ability to judge, understand, and analyze behaviors. At the end of the day, if you want to be successful and desire the ability to digest data, understand it quickly, and then apply it—you have to aspire to be interdisciplinary. This means diverse interests, being curious, reading and socializing outside of the given area you're exploring. Aspire to be a Renaissance man or woman. Train yourself to be able to have a capable conversation with anyone—no matter their career or level of education. Do that, and you'll find that doors open up for you.

Luck Is Bullshit

Opportunities are created by the way in which people interact with situations and justify their experiences. People with good luck didn't bathe in unicorn farts. They made well-informed decisions, said yes to opportunities, were open to tackling challenges, and didn't focus on how they were wronged or how lady luck neglected them. They face roadblocks or setbacks, bypass them, and forget about them. Luck is simply the result of moving forward with an equal blend of optimism, persistence, and situational intelligence.

Accept Failure

We all experience failure differently. The one truth that is the same for all of us is that we will inevitably fail. Some of those failures will be big, some of those failures will be small. However, it is easy to look at our own failures and to beat ourselves up over them. Often we look at those around us, or those we aspire to, or even those we dislike—and mark our successes and failures against theirs. This is an inescapable part of being human, it's also grossly misleading and a disservice to ourselves.

Why? Because people rarely advertise their failures. Even in the peer-reviewed academic world, there is a huge problem with misleading findings, not because the positive research isn't valid or good but because the failures—the negative findings or failed experiments—are rarely disclosed or talked about. It is painfully difficult, but the truth is that we learn the most from our failures. The issue isn't the failure itself. It is how we respond to it and what we do next.

As part of a deeply frustrating and prolonged job search in my late 20s, I trudged through numerous interviews. One of the most difficult questions to answer was the question, "Have you ever failed at something, and if so, what was it and how did you respond?". I knew that I had, of course, failed at things. But, as I sat wracking my brain I struggled to recall a failure of any consequence.

Eventually, I realized why—I've trained myself to learn what I can from a failure and then to put it behind me and to progress. It's no easy thing to do, and it took years of working on accepting that I cannot excel at everything and that there will be missteps. It wasn't until I truly delved into my past experiences that I was able to recall specific incidents. They remain uncomfortable for me to dwell on, but I also got what I needed from them.

The moral of the story? Don't ignore or pretend you didn't fail or make mistakes but at the same time don't get lost in self-pity or excessive over analysis. Accept that they are part of life and move forward.

One area I still struggle with is accepting a simple learned truth: the fear of failure is often significantly worse than the feeling of failure itself. Quite often we fail to chase opportunities, initiate conversations, or pursue opportunities out of a fear of what will happen and the judgment and horrible feeling that will ensue if we fail. The truth is that these are often grossly overstated and things rarely work out the way we imagine they will. Moreover, hesitation and fear that keep us from acting are often what facilitates and brings failure to fruition. I know this, I have accepted this, but I still have to fight myself on a regular basis to push past that fear and to pursue challenging or "risky" opportunities as they arise.

The Emotional Quotient

In fall of 2016, I found myself listening to a podcast interview on *The Tim Ferriss Show* with an individual who was brilliant but, at least earlier in his life, had a low Emotional Quotient (EQ). It was outlined as a balance and secondary aspect to IQ (Intelligence Quotient). One of the most interesting elements in the conversation included the high IQ/low EQ individual discussing how he had to teach himself to nurture his EQ.

We often take it for a given that in many cases high IQ/low EQ individuals simply are as they are. The observations in the podcast served as a spark, that ignited recognition of an observation that I'd been digesting and working over in my mind for a few years. Since the interview, I've come to see the, "it's just how they/I/you are" observation as an erroneous assumption. Instead, by taking a more flexible and fluid approach paired with introspection, I now see it as a powerful framework for exploring and understanding our own current level of EQ and how it should be nurtured to best suit our needs.

Shows like *Elementary* with its depiction of a modern day Sherlock Holmes and the Sherlock Holmes narrative as a whole focus on exploring this relationship. These shows, books, and stories highlight this progression by pairing an extremely high IQ individual with a well-balanced mid-level IQ/EQ individual who helps facilitate the low-EQ individual's emotional education. They often have the intellect and capacity to engage with the high IQ individual and garner their respect through understanding and accomplishment, but are individuals who also can then impart and serve as a framework for that individual to discover and implement their own emotional awareness and evolution.

Once you see these narratives through the high IQ/low EQ perspective it offers wonderful insights into the questions we can ask ourselves and those around us to better understand our own nature. How empathic are we? What sort of impulse control do we exhibit and in what aspects of our lives? How do I engage with the people around me? How aware am I of the ramifications of my actions on those I interact with and how can I modify my behaviors to make those more positive and less negative?

The challenges faced by extremely high IQ individuals and parallel ways of perception, thinking and communicating have always fascinated me. From autism to nurture-based conditions or just the frustration of a high IQ mind that operates in a fundamentally different way, the need to define and explore the EQ side of the equation is an incredible insight into how different brains work.

There's not much to add here, beyond encouraging you to consider your own EQ and then to use that as a way of better understanding the people you meet. I also tend to think it has far-reaching implications for questions of ethics and cultural norms. I find it tends to be directly linked to my interest and belief that empathy, not dogma, is the driving force that true morality comes from.

Imposter Syndrome

Though directly related to the bold generalist I mentioned above, one of the other areas that I've focused on working to counteract and combat heavily in recent years is impostor syndrome—that fundamental nagging doubt that both drives us but also leaves us constantly swinging in states of frustrated flux.

The sensation that we're impostors, that somehow we've fooled all those around us into thinking we're more capable, more gifted, more knowledgeable than we actually are and that at any minute that mistake will be revealed is an inherent challenge for most of us. This is particularly intense among those who have a well-balanced IQ and EQ. While I know it's normal, especially in peers, many of whom I've had numerous conversations with and who are individuals who I have the utmost respect and admiration for, it's no less easy to deal with.

As an expat, in a highly competitive market, with an unusual resume, I found myself torn between a desire to stay in Denmark and the very real opportunities located elsewhere. As part of that process, I applied to more than 150 companies, interviewed with 19 of which 4 took me to the final round only to choose the other candidate. For someone unfamiliar with failure, it was a deeply humbling experience that also led me to develop essential new behaviors and perspectives.

I've focused heavily on being diligent in categorizing my successes (recording them and making an actual list I can reference and refer back to) and stopping the emotional undercurrents that feed my own impostor syndrome in its tracks. I am always working to catch myself when I start to undermine myself or second guess, focusing instead on tallying my competencies. Acknowledging it for what it is. Compartmentalizing it. Using it as a natural and useful gut check to ensure I am doing the work I need to, to prepare myself, and then to dismiss the nagging uncertainty.

The result has been a fundamental shift in how I'm centered, respond to issues, and in my own belief in myself and my capability. Which isn't to say it's not still a daily struggle. But, it's now just one thread in a tapestry of motivations and inspirations which serve to push me forward toward new endeavors, challenges, and opportunities.

I find one of the most nefarious elements of imposter syndrome is the utter incoherence of it. I see it most often with my photography where I can, over the course of a week, get featured by National Geographic and then just a few days later entertain thoughts of abandoning photography completely out of frustration and dissatisfaction with photos I've captured using artificial reference points or an off-day shooting. Maintaining an archive that I can reference, scroll through, and remind myself with is a wonderful tool for stopping those negative behaviors early. It's also something that many success-oriented people tend to be extremely bad at creating as they are perpetually chasing the next task or achievement.

Embracing Intelligence

As is typical of most late-bloomers, I don't have particularly fond memories of middle school and high school. Over time I developed wonderful friends, but for the most part, I spent a lot of time struggling to fit in or was disinterested in playing the social games that often resulted in status and acceptance. I didn't go out of my way to like the latest band and was generally apathetic about spending money on name brand clothes and shoes.

Before the start of first grade, we moved from Colorado to Arizona. In Sedona, most classes were a blur until 5th grade when we set off for a year of family travel through Europe. 6th grade came with a return to a local charter school, and by 7th we were off again RVing the U.S. for a year. 8th grade was in the same city but at a different school than 6th and after graduation we relocated to a larger city roughly an hour away where I spent the duration of high school.

Three things came from this. The first was that creating and maintaining friendships was a bit of a challenge, especially when it came to breaking into social circles that had existed uninterrupted since preschool. The second was that due to the travels, intellectual parents, and having had the opportunity to see a larger slice of the world, the things that interested me and I wanted to discuss were ... well ... different than what was cool. Third, the change in schools and cities let me constantly tweak and hone who I was and wanted to be.

My interests were focused on history and long forgotten empires. On geeky topics and global issues which I'd discovered in conversations with adults over my two years on the road and wandering some of the world's most iconic museums. The people I got along best with were my teachers, which, while great from an academic perspective is usually relatively poisonous for social success. It didn't help that my passion to share what I was interested in and my experiences, combined with shyness and disdain for the high school forest party, made me come across as a bit arrogant and smug. For late bloomers and academics, this conundrum probably sounds familiar even if the reasons that led you there look a bit different.

But, with time, I realized that American society was in a period that relished and praised the archetypical dumb jock and penalized the nerd, the geek, and the intellectual. To some extent, I think we've seen that change in the last decade, but despite this positive pivot, it's still largely entrenched in our society. My parents explained it as a game and always encouraged me to look at the game, figure out what the rules were, and then decide how to play it.

Fair enough. With time I first figured out the game and refused to play, then eventually decided to strike a balance. The cost of that balance was downplaying and reducing my more intellectual interests, in favor of an external narrative that was more social. In its simplest form, it meant playing stupid or remaining silent. Passion, curiosity and a voracious hunger for knowledge are wonderful, but often it comes across as arrogant, cocky, geeky, or obnoxious, particularly at a young age.

In its simplest form, it meant instead of being the kid at the front of the class, with hand upraised wherever possible, I resigned myself to suffer in silence or moved myself further to the back. It meant adopting an approach that allowed me to perform and succeed but not to the extent that it put me in the spotlight, front and center, in a way that would create friction. It also meant coming to terms with the reality that many people would misinterpret my eagerness and excitement for arrogance or showboating. It would take years more before I learned that often, the delivery was irrelevant and that misinterpretation was more the triggering of their own insecurities or fears and embarrassment than anything within my control.

Over time I developed a mask. That mask was a persona I could slip into. One that spoke slightly less eloquently, that used a slightly more limited vocabulary, that avoided topics prone to triggering resentment or issues. But, with it, also came a certain level of avoidance. It became a motivation to be that A-/B+ student, instead of securing that A+. It became motivation to avoid the spotlight or to draw attention for the sake of humor or bravado instead of intellectual insights and raw achievement. And more than that, it became a reason to downplay and rapidly move on from successes and recognition tied to intellectual success instead of reveling in them.

Now, twenty years later, I still catch myself falling back into some of these techniques. Unfortunately, at a certain level, like any mask or persona, that identity eventually merges into who you are and how you see yourself. Even when you move beyond it, when you largely discard it, and as the world around you changes—the things that were rewarded in high school become irrelevant or even detrimental to success.

In general, this tends to take many forms. One that I often observed among my peers was among young women, particularly those who were particularly attractive. The iconic dumb blond stereotype was inevitably an oppressive weight which has been discussed at great lengths within elements of the feminist movement. At university, where I was participating in the honors college and surrounded by highly intelligent women, and later in the professional workplace, it often created a web of significant insecurities and confused identities. Similar to my experience, but in a much more potent and vitriolic way, intelligent women often subconsciously found the best way to success was to obscure their intelligence, downplay the expression of that intelligence and turn up the outward bimbo.

The challenge becomes that even when you tell yourself that you're protecting your inner focus and identity, and only playing a role, doing so is impossible. That mask truly does become part of you and your own self-voice. While it lubricates general social interactions when it comes to things like dating it ultimately creates inferior relationships. While you may be able to attract a wider cross section of potential partners, some of whom you can then truly convert and engage with at a more intellectual level, it also tends to add a lot of static, replacing quality interactions and good fit with general noise.

It's also both exciting and frustrating that, over time, the metrics for success necessarily pivot and reverse. That as we advance into our twenties, thirties and beyond, those who intellectually excel and own their intelligence have a tendency to outperform those who never developed it, were less capable, or who sought to downplay those abilities. I hope that over time we get better at educating students about the importance of striking a balance and developing proper social skills, but also fully nurturing and embracing their curiosity and intellect. The amount of angst, agonies, and hopelessness, as well as emotional scarring and complex baggage that marks many of the world's most successful people, relates back directly to the challenges that arise in striking this balance.

It's also clear that many either lose themselves fully and just leave the mask on permanently, are broken, or never manage to acknowledge and then do the self-work to properly discard that mask or overcome the insecurities or low-output behaviors that result. As you navigate your own journey, I encourage each of you to consider your own path, your own narrative, and how that has evolved in recent years—or, if you're still early in that process—the direction that you're eager to chart.

As I reflect on where I am in my own personal journey, I fully appreciate and value the ability to engage in the less serious or more casual. I've come to understand the social value that shared experiences and commentary on things like fashion or art or music bring and how they help us find similar people and to form valuable in-groups. At the same time, I've also come to focus on being more transparent in embracing my curious and intellectual self and less apologetic about it. I still endeavor to strike a balance that brings with it humility and curiosity, not knowledge weaponized for social impact absent the ability to engage with and learn from everyone.

Temptation to Self-Sabotage

One of the greatest predictors of success isn't if an individual is capable or lucky. It's their ability to master the temptation to self-sabotage. The temptation to self-sabotage is there for all of us. In some cases, it's more overt, like not showing up for a final exam or waiting too long to respond to a job offer. In other cases, it's far less obvious, like the successful entrepreneur who makes rash decisions or takes actions subconsciously designed to sabotage and negate their success.

At its heart, the temptation to self-sabotage is born out of fear and uncertainty. It's the feeling of loss of control, of racing at speed beyond what we're comfortable with, and plunging into the unknown. It is, at a certain level, an attempt to slam on the brakes. That sense of primal fear ends up being so strong that we find ourselves self-sabotaging. This happens even when we know that it'll return us to a state that will be bad for us, embarrassing, painful, and potentially leave us even worse off than if we had pushed forward.

One of the essential skills that differentiates people who are consistent performers is their ability to identify, master and then act in opposition to self-sabotage. If you're a student, this means taking careful steps not to miss exams and to read directions. It also includes keeping your ego in check and ensuring that you don't self-sabotage through bluster, pride or arrogance. If you're applying for a job, this means ensuring you take the steps needed to prepare your resume and then taking the key steps to send it—paying special attention to things like timing or typos tied to the business and its name or focus. If you're already in a job, it means doing your work diligently, and ensuring that when the visible moments come, that the fear of being put on the spot, having your talent recognized or having the spotlight focused on you doesn't lead you to self-sabotage. This can be overt or more subtle; from suddenly being unprepared to neglecting the details that appear to be out of your control but are truthfully just a matter of preparation.

In practice, consider an individual that decides to prepare for his first marathon. As part of that preparation, it's important that the individual run regularly, building stamina. The individual does, getting in shape and hitting good times. But, as the date approaches, nerves build, and the individual has another social event. For the event the individual decides to buy and wear a pair of new dress shoes, fully aware that the shoes will inevitably damage his feet. Fast forward to the following morning, with two weeks to go to the marathon, the individual wakes up with bloody blisters on the backs of both feet. There's now just enough time for the blisters to mostly heal before the marathon, but the individual has subconsciously created an excuse to stop running and drop out of the race. At best, his performance will be reduced significantly confirming his fears. At worst, he drops out completely using the injury as justification.

The truth of it is, even when we're aware of the temptation to self-sabotage, we aren't completely successful in squelching it and mastering it. The reality is that no matter how long you work to master that voice, it always remains there and always requires your attentiveness to ensure you don't let it sneak out to undercut you. But, when you do that, when you accept it for what it is, just another part of our process, when you clearly catch yourself starting to engage in a self-sabotaging behavior and then act immediately to negate it, you will chart a path toward success.

When people state that they create their own luck, in truth what they're saying is that they master their initial temptation to self-sabotage and embrace opportunities that present themselves that they'd otherwise be blind to. Learn to master that temptation to self-sabotage and to say yes to opportunities and you'll rapidly see major changes in how you engage and interact with the world.

Internalization of Self-Confidence

As the final years of high school began I decided I had had enough of my crippling shyness and social anxiety. Over time, I began to work aggressively on crafting and mastering my ability to be at ease in a social environment. With time and effort, I effectively did so.

What resulted was the ability to operate socially with confidence and to project self-confidence to those around me. Whether it was taking the stage for a presentation or making a social introduction at a party or gathering, I had managed to build an external self-confidence that was effective, persuasive, and compelling.

When people looked at or engaged with me, they saw someone who was able to exude self-confidence in most aspects of his behavior. From casual body language to social protocol these were all complemented by a track record of documented professional successes which we commonly associate with self-confidence.

Often, as people talk about self-confidence, this is the extent to which they delve into the topic. At some levels, it's the classic actor's dilemma. How can an individual on stage or on screen play some of the most confident and successful people in the world but suddenly harbor self-doubt or lack confidence when they return to their true identity and self?

For those familiar with academic communication theory, Goffman's concept of front and back stage no doubt comes to mind. In this theory, the two aspects of our self are explored using the concept of the front stage where we perform for others and the backstage where we can be our true self, without guard or pretense.

In my case, it was only as I graduated from my Bachelors and took my three-month solo walkabout through Europe that I began to realize that the social confidence I had crafted and mastered was wonderful but not fully internalized. This is to say that while I was confident, and that impacted my behavior, my relationships, and how I engaged with people, at heart I was still very much that self-doubting, insecure, profoundly socially uncomfortable eleven-year old.

As I charted my own path during those three

months, I found myself in situation after situation where I had no option but to act to solve my own problems and to believe in myself. In those moments, I wasn't able to attribute the success to the people around me. I wasn't able to leverage my social support network to bail me out. In those moments it was up to me to act, to make a decision, to pursue it to its end, and to then evaluate the result.

It was only when I returned from the trip, sat down, and reflected on what had happened and how I had changed that I started to realize just how different externalized self-confidence is from truly internalized self-confidence. To internalize self-confidence is to master and re-educate the inner voice that whispers in our ear. It is to know we can do something, to know we have done something, to find acceptance of that, and to take ownership in our own internal narrative of the realities of that ability and success.

Nearly six years later I returned to Arizona for a month and found myself sitting in the living room at one of my mentor's homes. I was two years into my MA in Denmark and more than three years had passed since my solo trip to Europe. As we sat, and chatted, he made a comment that caught me off guard, "You seem much more at ease with yourself." At first, I wasn't sure how to take it. It was obviously intended as a compliment, but did it imply I had been weak, uppity or doubting before? Was I now coming across as arrogant? Or was it something else.

With reflection, I quickly realized that, in practice, I was and that it was a wonderful observation.

The process of internalizing my self-confidence, of discovering who I was, and how I chose to relate to the world was something that was gradually progressing over time. What he had picked up on, and commented upon was the transition that took that internalized self-confidence and competence I had developed and pulled it into the essence of who I am.

To this day there are still a plethora of areas where I struggle to align the two. From dating and relationships to taking the stage for presentations and certain types of social settings, there is still significant work to be done. But, through it all, I've come to realize and accept that what skills I want to perfect and eventually internalize, began on that externalized front stage, but then over time had to be incorporated into my core identity.

It's only once we've done that work, that we've truly internalized and built a strong core, that we can act and believe in ourselves in a way that empowers and enables us.

Success Can Be Lethal

Success and intelligence are wonderful partners. Ask most highly intelligent, motivated or successful people what traits they value most, and their intelligence and the identity that goes with it will feature prominently. Similarly, as we achieve in life we're also defined by, motivated, and incredibly proud of those achievements.

If you thumb through the obituaries for individuals who committed suicide, time and time again one of the things that stands out is that, in many cases, these were profoundly successful individuals. These are often people with a strong drive, with a long string of accomplishments, and with an extended social network heavily invested in and involved with that individual.

What often gets overlooked and seldom talked about are the dynamics which weigh heavily on highly motivated and successful people. With performance and accomplishment comes an innate expectation from those around you that you will always continue to perform. For the A+ student with perfect grades, who has constantly received feedback from parents and peers about how impressed and proud they are of the individual for that performance—the thought of suddenly disappointing all these people becomes a very real and substantial weight.

With success and high performance comes the narrative that you will constantly go on and succeed, excel, and accomplish great things. While those challenges, tasks, and accomplishments are relevant to the individual, that sense and weight of responsibility to everyone else often becomes a heavy yoke. The individual not only harbors their own internal expectations, but also comes to embody and feel responsible for the investment in time, energy, money, and love from their network and peers.

Which is why, when suddenly some aspect of that identity comes crashing down, it has the potential to break people. That fear of failing everyone around you, of having to explain why you didn't succeed or continue down the path that they anticipated, can rapidly far outweigh the realities of the situation which are often far less dire.

In the West, we're often shocked by the high suicide rates in places like Japan. We also often scornfully disparage the concept of face, and find ourselves in disbelief that a loss of face can drive even the most successful CEO to commit suicide.

Yet, the underlying social mechanism is the same. That mechanism also breaks many people in the West. We don't call it a loss of face, and we don't have a series of integrated social protocols that magnify the lethality of the issue. But, we do have tens of thousands of suicides and attempted suicides in the U.S. each year, many of which are triggered by that sense of lost face and of failing your community of peers and family. All of which doesn't even begin to tally the intense emotional fear, depression, and angst that ravages hundreds of thousands each year at a deeply impactful, if less lethal, level.

As people who strive toward success, who are surrounded by peers who similarly harbor many of the traits of successful high achievers, it is important that we step back and we remember not to lose context. Far too often people confuse their social network and peer's excitement about their success and performance for an expectation that they follow a specific track or maintain a specific success trajectory.

In practice, when a crisis hits and that A+ streak is broken, or the door to a professional career is closed due to an accident, failed test, or bad decision, they will not only understand but continue to respect and support you.

Meanwhile as friends, as peers, as parents and as other individuals deeply invested in those we care about, it's similarly important that we are aware of what kind of feedback we are giving to those around us. It's important not to expect perfection from even the most capable and skilled among us. It's also important to remember that even our heroes are human.

In its totality, it's essential that we, as individuals, remember that success and achievement are the sum of our experiences and contributions in life. It's not something defined by a singular event or moment in time. It's for that reason that failure or disappointment to one small area of our total contribution can actually serve as an essential foundation for our future successes. The only occasion where we truly lose and end up disappointing those that matter most to us is when we prematurely deprive ourselves of the opportunity to fully embrace our true potential.

Stare down the fear of failing those around you. Tally and take account of your successes. Relish the new opportunity to experiment. Recognize that all situations are fluid and solutions always exist that provide entirely new approaches to the same opportunities.

Skepticism and the Scientific Method

One of the most critical and prolific threats to success out there is a misunderstanding or fundamentally absent understanding of the scientific method. At its heart the scientific method is a way of observing the world around us. From those observations we create potential explanations. Then, we do everything we possibly can to prove those explanations wrong. If you can't—then, until someone can do so in a documented and proven way—it's accepted as a likely truth. In this way, everyone who employs the scientific method is a skeptic. But they're a skeptic that applies that skepticism even-handedly and with a focus on documented, fact-based results, not their agenda or what they set out to prove. As soon as you do that, you've drifted into pseudo-skepticism which is deeply damaging. Pseudo-skepticism is alive and well, prolific and loves to act in the guise of critical inquiry and genuine skepticism.

Unfortunately, the allure of semi-accurate information, or information taken out of context, all viewed without the lens of the genuine scientific method, creates fools of people on both sides particularly in the political spectrum. The real draw of pseudo-skepticism is that it gives you the impression that you have a special secret, that you're smarter than everyone else, and it gives you access to a social in-group which has a relatively simple rule of entry: belief in the narrative. Often, it also comes in the form of wanting to confirm and put the authority of someone we respect or want to respect above what the existing evidence states, or just being eager to have a secret and to be an early adopter.

While unhealthy in our personal lives, this can also be profoundly dangerous in a business context. Consider what happens when we fail to follow the basic scientific method and instead allow ourselves to be misled by what we want to believe, or a consensus view that is beneficial to our narrative. Similarly, it's one thing to make a decision. It's another to make that decision without doing the legwork or informing yourself at an appropriate level. Telling yourself it's actually fact, and that the other information available is inherently wrong, leads to bad decision making and costly mistakes.

The other key trait when engaging pseudo-skepticism is to rely on fundamentally debunked and flawed sources which in turn generate skepticism about high-quality sources. Here again, it's often based in poorly selecting the authority which you're going to pull from, and failing to make a complete and in-depth review and analysis utilizing the scientific method.

At the heart of it, is genuinely asking why. Not once, not twice, but repeatedly. As important, it means listening to the answer when that's given and then doing the leg work to validate that answer.

If I tell you gravity is real, you're justified in asking why. If I tell you that it's because scientific consensus has found it to be real. You're again justified in asking why. At which point, when I explain to you gravitational theory and the basic elements that are completely replicable, you're once again justified in asking why.

At a certain point, however, it's essential that you look at the situation and make a decision. Either, you invest the time to educate yourself fully and put yourself in a position where you have the complete degrees and resources to test the theory at a highly advanced level, or you accept the scientifically, peer-reviewed, repeatedly-tested results from the most credible sources available. This includes an assessment of the source, those individuals (and preferably teams of individuals) who have taken that action.

Of course, in simple cases like gravity, you can also avoid much of that by deploying a simple test for bullshit: Take a rock. Hold it above your head. Let go of it. You'll quite quickly confirm gravity is very, very real.

What tends to lead people astray in this process, however, is how scientific "fact" evolves. This stems from different uses of the same term. When I state something is a fact in day-to-day life, say, to describe that at 10:00 A.M. on Tuesday the 23rd of 2020 I have ten fingers, that's easily confirmed and concrete. It's essentially either a false statement or a fact. That's also not going to change, even if at 10:01 A.M. I grow an 11th finger.

When we use the scientific method we're operating using the concept of scientific fact or, if being more technically correct, a scientific theory. Scientific theory in this context isn't the same as blindly guessing that the woman in blue sitting next to you likes cherries. Scientific theory, like the theory of gravity, is a theory that was proposed, which has then been researched by a large number of different people, analyzing a large number of different data sets, which can be concretely replicated without generating data that disagrees with or is different from what the theory states. At this point, to differentiate between a general theory—the blue sky makes me happy the bluer it is— and scientific theory—gravity is real and is 9.807 m/s^2 —the term scientific fact gets used.

In cases where there is so much evidence, over such an extended period of time, and the resulting observation is relatively straight forward and consistent, these highly proven scientific theories become perceived as unchangeable fact. But, the part that throws people is that through the scientific method, there is no such thing as an absolute fact. The scientific method is perpetually open to new inputs and data that updates the scientific model /theory initially put in place.

But, that doesn't mean that some random study by some unqualified individual that pops up magically immediately overturns what was previously held as scientific fact. Why? Because the burden of proof then sits with that individual to show that their new data is superior in quality and corrects an issue with the existing data. Why? Because in most cases, that new data? It's different because there was a critical error with it and that new data has to be scrutinized for validity and application by the scientific community.

Another way to consider the scientific approach is that it's essentially an algorithm that is constantly testing new alternatives to refine and improve the efficiency and accuracy of the equation. Each new piece of information gets tested to see if it's valid. Even if it seems valid initially, over the long-term, it may turn out not to be and is rejected.

The real problem arises when you have individuals who skip steps, fake information, or build research on top of existing scientifically confirmed data, which misunderstand the source data or omit fundamental pieces. This is often seen in research intentionally designed to be biased toward a predetermined outcome (e.g.; Tobacco or Sugar industry-funded research). From there, when best practices and audits aren't properly performed by qualified people you continue a narrative that may sound good, but ultimately ends up being not only inaccurate but harmful.

This is ultimately what happened with the current vaccines-cause-autism conspiracy theories and the currently hot topic that leads some to reject humanity's impact on climate change. In the case of the vaccines, the initial evidence was faked but still managed to get published triggering paranoia of a cover up. But, those most interested in the cover-up narrative are those who simultaneously reject and refuse to deep dive into the original research, the flaws with it, or to fully evaluate follow up research and updated data. In short, they've replaced objective skepticism and the application of the scientific method with pseudo-skepticism.

Human-impacted climate change is more complex. Largely because the sum of the factors in play is also infinitely more sophisticated, making the science harder to confirm and understand on an individual level and easier to misquote and misrepresent by malicious actors. Much of that science also contradicts convenient religious and industrial narratives, which has led to an incredible amount of money trying to inject false information into the algorithm. But ultimately, as the science is based on replicability and multiple simultaneous models, scientific consensus ends up being reached and maintained.

While this science is still developing, and not at a level of refinement with a data set robust enough to answer all aspects of what is occurring or to predict effects proactively, it does provide an in-depth and highly accurate overview, which in this case also passes a basic logic test. That logic test is to dig into the heat island effect—how large paved cities change weather patterns—and to do a bit of light research on places like the Aral Sea, which was an inland sea drained completely by humans.

This is also where a critical but genuine respect for academic experts with specialized expertise is important. In the same way, we wouldn't trust a taxi driver with a cabbie's license to pilot a 1,500-foot tanker because they're both "professional drivers with licenses," academic credentials are similarly not interchangeable. The assurance from a Ph.D. in Chemistry is not interchangeable on climate-related issues with that of a Ph.D. in Climate Science who also has a proven track record of doing effective science. Notably, in this equation, even a Master's in Climate Science with proven research history, is significantly more qualified than the Ph.D. in Chemistry. This is an obvious and necessary result of specialization. Postgraduate education does not consist of general courses common to all disciplines.

At the end of the day, there have always been snake oil salesmen. These individuals play on our hopes, they play on our desire to believe, and are skilled at crafting complex stories or using a magician's flair for misdirection to divert our attention.

When it comes to charting our way through life, through business, and in making daily decisions—it's imperative that we understand and act in a way that utilizes the critical tools offered by the scientific method. Not only for understanding the world around us and making a decision, but also for constantly re-evaluating, updating, and enhancing our own internal narrative and beliefs.

In all aspects of our lives, we should be skeptical and embrace skepticism. But it should be skepticism based in curiosity and the pursuit of knowledge, not agenda, emotion, or to validate some secondary position we hold.

We are also at our strongest when we take a scientific approach to fact and the things we consider absolute in our lives. We must always strive to be open to new inputs, even those that fundamentally change things we believe to be absolute. But, we need only worry about it when the evidence itself merits it.

Thinking Ahead or Jumping In

Different people have different ways of interacting with the world around them. Some are almost completely immediate and impulsive in how they navigate through life. For these individuals, issues regularly arise as unintended side effects of their actions inevitably correspond to decisions or actions taken with little to no long-term perspective taken into account.

At the other end of the spectrum, you have people fundamentally paralyzed by the wide range of potential outcomes each decision might have. These individuals, not unlike the world's best chess players, see a multi-dimensional world that is infinitely complex with each fresh action setting off a series of dominoes leading to a complex combination of hypothetical results.

In recent months I've taken this a bit further by visually picturing rings emanating out in front of myself. I picture each of these rings as different time *or* activity intervals. The individual operating in a purely impulsive state would perpetually act in the first while the mental chess player would chart a path twenty-plus rings out. From there, I have started to explore how I interact with situations and how the people around me interact with the same situation.

For example, I find myself walking up the stairs with a friend late at night. I live on the fourth floor, the stairs can be quite loud, and the doors are relatively thin—all knowledge we're both aware of. Yet, as we make our way up the stairs, we're both functioning from two very different states of awareness. For her, she's operating in the first or second circle. Her focus is on scaling the steps and our conversation, blind or oblivious to the greater context and potential impact of our footfalls.

At the same time, I have a tendency to fall towards the further end of the spectrum. I share her focus as we make the way up the stairs, but also can't help but consider several added levels beyond the immediate impulsive focus on the moment. As I talk in hushed tones, she responds in a normal street voice. As I take quiet steps, she takes loud steps that echo through the stairwell. I find my mind flinching in annoyance, concerned that we're disrupting the neighbors and taking it one step further, also weighing that those disturbed or annoyed neighbors may be less tolerant and short-tempered in the future.

It's not that she's inconsiderate or that if I pointed out the issues she would object to being quieter. It's just a matter of perspective and her way of relating and interacting to the world around her. In this particular case, my more long-term perspective helps me avoid the creation of future issues and gives me added insight into some, if not all, of the ramifications of certain behaviors or actions.

But, consider another situation. This time, I find myself out on a double date. The date is progressing. The energy and vibe are positive. All four people seem to be on the same wavelength. The chemistry is good. Yet, my friend and I differ significantly. In this case, my friend and his date both end up being more impulsive and immediate people while my date and I are not.

We finish our drinks. We go for a walk. We split into couples and give each other space. The friend and his date rapidly throw themselves into a deep kiss and enjoy the moment without being overly concerned about what comes next or what's going on around them. Simultaneously, my date and I share the same chemistry and attraction but instead settle into conversation. In our minds, an awareness of the people walking past every few minutes weighing on our minds paired with other considerations. Do I try and kiss her? I don't want to make her uncomfortable. Is she ready? What expectation does she have for where the evening will lead. Are we compatible enough to consider a second date, or is it better to avoid the kiss now and bypass the awkwardness of not having an interest in a follow-up?

In both examples, different ways of relating have different costs and benefits. But, as importantly, they also explain fundamental differences in behavior and provide what, for me at least, has become a wonderful way of understanding people and their actions. When trying to explain why you did or didn't do something or why something annoys you or excites you, it's often incredibly frustrating and difficult if the other person interacts with and moves through the world differently. It can also be incredibly awkward. Just imagine the moments where you're simultaneously in sync and completely out of sync. An easy example that a lot of 20 and 30 somethings face? Laying in bed negotiating with an impulsive partner about why you refuse to have sex without a condom on despite their assurances that they've recently been tested for STDs.

Now, consider where you fall on the spectrum. Imagine a number of situations—both positive and negative—that span from relationships, to work, to how you learn, to when you lost your last phone. It's likely that you fall somewhere in the middle—but are you more impulsive or oriented more to a long-term perspective? Are you much further to one extreme or the other?

For added perspective and an easier diagnosis, also consider two people you get along with well and two who drive you absolutely crazy and consider where they might fall on the spectrum. Next time you find yourself in a conversation with each, keep in mind where the friction or smoothness comes from.

It sounds like a small thing, but ultimately, changing and understanding how we operate serves as a wonderful way for us to change how we interact, to plan more proactively, and to overcome decision paralysis. It's also a wonderful way to become more tolerant of the people around you and to help diminish destructive or counter-productive behaviors that are often costly or physically harmful.

The Pay It Forward Approach to Relationships

Shortly after completing my bachelor's degree I was working for a small mergers and acquisitions group as an analyst. This brought with it the possibility to potentially secure a bonus or a considerable referral if a company I introduced led to a completed deal. Fast forward to a birthday party for a friend of a friend whose dad was an extremely successful businessman. He was friendly, welcoming and before long asked a few questions about what I was doing and about me.

The correct course of action would have been to politely answer the questions, chat, and to engage on an individual level. But, feeling the overpowering sense that this was an opportunity I should be taking advantage of, I instead clumsily stumbled into what became a quasi-answer, quasi-pitch and ended with me fishing around and handing him a business card.

Even as I fumbled forward, I could feel the alarm bells in my mind going off—this wasn't me, this wasn't right, this wasn't how I engage. And as I handed him the business card, which he was gracious and polite enough to take in stride, I could see his body language change. While there's always a small sliver of a chance it might have worked, it wasn't worth it and more than that, it wasn't the right thing to do. I'd betrayed the cardinal rule of true networking, at a casual level violated his hospitality and the trust and inclusion of my friends. In so doing, I also turned what should have been a social moment into a poorly executed business pitch. All, while we were there to celebrate his daughter.

I always go back to and recall this moment because of the sheer cringe-worthiness of it. At that moment I'd degraded myself to the used-car salesman. Something that was fundamentally in opposition to how I believe in relating to people in general and most definitely how I believe effective and ethical business is done.

The truth is that while this type of business card pushing networking is common, especially if you consider certain industries, types of jobs and things like conferences, it's incredibly ineffective. It takes many forms. Sometimes it's running around and handing out business cards. Other times, it's adding random strangers by the hundreds on LinkedIn. In other cases, it's ignoring context, setting and the other person's needs in favor of pushing your pitch. "This is my moment, be bold!" overrides common decency and delivering genuine value, and the result is ordinarily the exact opposite of what you anticipated.

When I encounter "power networkers" or people who overtly approach me to "network" alarm bells go off left and right. These are often people that can't be trusted, that miss and lack social cues, that are absolutely self-centered and absorbed, that are liabilities, and that will inevitably make unreasonable requests or expect that they're entitled to my time or help. Last week I had one who had snuck into my Facebook circle through a social event send me a chat message to catch up. The catch was, it was obviously intentionally sent to me, but he'd failed to properly update the name from his copy-paste spam message. In so doing he crystallized my desire to avoid anything remotely business related tied to him.

Be Sincere

This gets to the core point of effective business and social networking in general. Be it for business, academia, dating, or life in general, be authentic and be sincere. Ultimately, the path to truly being successful in all social aspects of your life is to focus on engaging with people in a way that respects them as an individual with their own merits and value.

Sincerity and sound intention is something that transcends all other aspects of a social or professional relationship. When you're sincere, it doesn't matter if you're talking to someone radically more successful, wealthy or powerful than you—or, vice versa. The same also applies to age and engaging and interacting across generational or cultural lines.

When you genuinely and sincerely express curiosity and interest about an individual, you're making an investment in them and inviting the same. You're also positioning yourself to interact in a direct capacity with that individual outside of pretext. You're building rapport, you're learning what really matters and makes the individual work, and discovering what sort of compatibility there is between you as individuals.

Be Helpful

While the first step to richer relationships with people is being sincere, the second is to be helpful. The film *Pay It Forward* captured elements of the beauty, elegance, and profound impact positive actions have. Beyond that, I also often mentally visualize it as a stone cast into a still lake. The opportunity to have a positive impact sends out ripples and encourages similarly positive behavior that affects all aspects that you come into contact with.

Another way to consider it is as basic social sanitation. Consider what happens if people suddenly started throwing all trash onto the street with no thought to the people around them or long-term impact. Purely caught up in the immediate need and convenience of disposal. Simultaneously, consider what happens if that littering is then compounded by the lack of janitors cleaning up and constantly maintaining the common space. Before long, what was convenience and led to immediate gratification is replaced by filth and with time powerfully unpleasant aromas and then disease. The way we interact with the people around us is no different. Beyond that, not only is it essential that we aren't littering, but that we also assume, to some degree, the role of that communal janitor.

But, even more than that, when we act with sincerity and strive to be helpful in whatever capacity we can dedicate time and energy—we not only invest in the people around us, we enrich ourselves. Elsewhere I reference the popular concept which states, "We are the sum of the five people we surround ourselves with." At the heart of this concept is the very real infusion of ideas, energies, and the impact on our world view and emotional state that the people we surround ourselves with have on us.

Being helpful where and when you can, to the extent which you can, with as many people as you can, is an extension of this same core principle, just at a more watered-down level. Think of it as a secondary ring of inspirational influence which encircles the ring created by those primary five highly influential confidants.

I find that the reward I get in exchange for my time is a constant infusion of insights into new ways of thinking, exposure to exciting ideas, the opportunity to clarify and reflect on my own knowledge/experiences, and most important of all, to pay back the help that countless people have given me.

I suspect that growing up with two educators as parents played a pivotal role in illustrating the power of helping and inspiring. Through them, I've been able to see the incredible potential impact offering help can have. Beyond the actual action in the moment, offering to help sends a profound message of interest and investment in an individual that has the potential to rock them to their core. Even profoundly small things or single sentences of advice can play a pivotal role in shaping people's lives. You rarely know. More involved interactions, such as those of mentoring or teaching can alter the course of someone's life and stand out as vivid and influential memories decades later.

Feedback: Be Honest But Kind

I tend to think that one of the most profoundly challenging skills to master is the art of giving feedback. While as a culture we often focus quite heavily on how to receive feedback, which is equally important, very little input is dedicated to how to deliver feedback. In far too many instances people opt for one extreme or the other. This is to say, they either only provide positive feedback, often even when it's not sincere, or they hide behind hundred percent honesty.

Positive-only feedback is virtually worthless. It's the embodiment of that high school or college group paper-editing session where you had to rely on your classmates to offer you critical feedback on your paper—only to get back one circled typo for show and no substantive comments. The unfortunate reality is that your end product hasn't improved and the process of going through the farce of getting feedback wastes valuable time and energies that you could have spent refining the actual project.

At the same time, in recent years the concept of complete honesty has become increasingly popular. For some, this stems from an inability to read people and a relatively low EQ. For others, it's an easy excuse to offer the critical feedback they're interested in giving, but also gives them a curtain to hide behind. In so doing, they couch what is generally feedback or opinionated observation as concrete fact and in absolute terms without credence to context. The lack of nuance, admitting the inherent opinion that is embedded in feedback, and confusing feedback for commentary are all key issues that shape this approach. Also, understanding that when it is delivered in such a tactless, cruel, and oblivious way the core message and intended value never actually reach the receiver. The ultimate level of efficacy then ends up being on par with an individual who only offers positive feedback.

Ultimately, the best type of feedback is feedback that aspires to understand the receiver. That couches the material being provided in a way that is relatable, that is clear, that is constructive but which is still critical. Providing details and explaining the context or your own reasoning as to why something doesn't quite work or needs improvement or refinement involves more work and consideration from your end, but ultimately also provides an avenue for far better input. As an extension of this, it's also important to listen to, and let the individual, where applicable, explain and talk through your feedback. This helps them to better understand it and to discuss a path towards resolving the challenges you've highlighted.

Compete with Yourself, not Your Colleagues

One of the most poisonous types of environments is one which fosters and encourages a hyper-competitive atmosphere designed to pit classmate vs. classmate, friend vs. friend, or colleague vs. colleague. The performance logic seems straightforward enough on paper—if you create competition you'll ensure the best candidate secures the final spot or the reward.

In practice, however, that's usually not the actual result. Instead, you encourage candidates to dehumanize each other, to engage in a more limited function, while also eroding their own inner empathy. You foster the creation of us vs. them in-groups and you create an environment that encourages individuals to cheat or bend the rules in any way possible. It's a race to the bottom.

While this type of setup is often couched as Darwinian, the truth is, that true Darwinism actually highlights exactly why this doesn't work. Groups that create social and collaborative structures are fundamentally more effective than those that are purely individualistic and operate strictly out of self-interest. Humanity's prolific spread is the direct result of the mastery of our individualistic traits and the ability to constructively work collectively. Survival of the fittest is far too often mischaracterized as the strongest or the most capable in a one-dimensional sense. This fails miserably to actually understand the true nature and definition of fitness.

The path to a successful life and career that doesn't leave a trail of burned bridges and salt-sown relational minefields behind you is one in which you compete against yourself. Your goal should not be to beat down, to sabotage, to block or to undermine everyone around you. It should be to chart a course where you constantly aspire to deliver your personal best, and then improve upon it.

To truly perform and succeed it's important that you constantly learn from what you've already accomplished. It's important that you delve into and explore in honest terms what you need to do to improve. It's also pivotally important that you explore and have honest self-talk on what you're willing to do to accomplish certain things, if that trade-off is worth it, and if it gets you closer to a goal that's worth attaining. Do that and you will not only find yourself excelling, you'll also find yourself charting a much more aerodynamic course where obstacles and detrimental relationships are far less impactful, not of your own making, and slide by without dragging you down.

The challenge here is in doing it in a healthy fashion. In other chapters, I touch upon Imposters Syndrome and the need to document our success. I also highlight other character and personality traits that are common among highly intelligent and motivated people. At a certain level, when you challenge and compete with yourself, you have to remember to let yourself win while simultaneously reminding yourself to be a gracious winner. Often, we walk far too harshly in our own minds.

Deliver Value and Don't Keep Score

"Now you owe me one" remains one of the most cringe-worthy ways of socializing in existence. While a tit-for-tat approach is ubiquitous and can be used to explain why men send unsolicited dick pics to political campaigners turned appointees post-election, it remains a vile way to interact. Which isn't to say that at some level all social interactions don't have a transactional element—they do. It's also not to say that there aren't situations where it's important to identify individuals that ask, and ask, and ask, but are never available to offer support or return a favor.

Ultimately though, when you find people that are

primarily incentivized by building up favors as currency, alarm bells should start to sound. Why? Because as soon as you transactionalize helping the people around you, you've clearly sent the message that you're not going to invest in helping them succeed, unless it's directly beneficial to you. Which, is not only shortsighted, it also makes it crystal clear that you can't be relied upon and that in a pinch, you're likely to go missing.

The most successful people, who ethically navigate the complexities of life and business, are individuals that are reasonable with their time and what they offer other people, but who do it freely. These are individuals whose primary concern is that when they do decide to offer to help, that you respect their time by being prepared, diligent, and having thought out what you need help with. These are also individuals less concerned with reclaiming some favor down the road, and more concerned with investing in you and helping you succeed, fully confident that as that happens positive interactions follow naturally.

But, if they don't? That's fine as well. As long as you pay it forward in some other capacity, it all comes back to the positive ripple theory—the impact you have going forward improves all aspects of the ecosystem, in turn, feeding back with both people benefiting.

It's impossible to be successful without input and feedback from countless individuals. It's of fundamental importance that you are constantly aware of the pivotal role random kindness plays. The same goes for the impact of people who didn't have to help you and didn't anticipate you'd be able to repay them in some way but, decided to help you anyway.

Impress people with your investment in them. Help them succeed and you won't have to keep score. You'll have fostered a wonderfully constructive relationship that leaves them equally excited to be involved in projects with you. That is far more valuable than any single favor or tallied request.

Nordic Cultural Insights into Communication

Silence and gaps in conversation are something deeply uncomfortable for the average American. Yet, for many other cultures, they're a natural, and at times, even an essential part of the conversation. In your typical American conversation, you'll rarely find such a thing as a comfortable silence, a reflective silence, or a natural silence. For the average American in a normal conversation, there's really only one type of silence, and that is awkward silence.

Before moving to Denmark and ending up immersed in Nordic culture, it's not something I noticed or was really aware of. From an early age, Americans are taught that an awkward silence is a conversational cataclysm and something to avoid at all costs. This approach makes sense in an American context. In large part, the American conversational approach can best be described as conversational layering. Each individual is rapidly engaging with the other, quickly layering on new overlapping information in rapid succession. Add in the fast-paced rapid-fire approach to speaking common among most Americans, and you've laid the groundwork for a completely unexpected cultural clash.

Unlike Americans, Nordics and Scandinavians (I'll just say Nordics moving forward) have a conversational culture which treasures the silences. This comes from a significantly increased comfort with silence compared to their American counterparts. Nordics have a very turn-based structure and style. While the Finnish are notorious for the slow pacing of their conversations and their extreme comfort with what would otherwise be considered painfully uncomfortable periods of silence, it is a trend present to a lesser extent across all of the Nordic countries. The result is a conversational practice with definite gaps to signify the closure of a point. In this way, a traditional Nordic conversation more closely resembles the structure of a formal debate rather than a round table free-for-all discussion.

Due to the near bilingualism of most Nordic citizens and the fact that many also speak American English with very mild accents, it is very easy for non-native speakers to forget that the Nordics are still not quite native speakers. This means that when the silences occur during the natural flow of a conversation, they are amplified because of the added need to process, digest, and periodically search for missing words. Something further compounded when talking with native English speakers due to our heavy use of regional slang and provincial idioms.

In discussions with Danish friends and by closely exploring my own conversations, I've come to realize that this translates into a certain level of frustration among Nordics when talking with native English speakers. It can often translate into the perception that the American (or another native speaker) is arrogant, dismissive, not paying attention, and/or rude.

Keeping in mind the two conversational styles I mentioned previously, here are a few areas where I've watched some issues arise.

Affirmation Behavior

A common American practice to show continued engagement with a conversation is to give constant positive feedback. This can either be gestural (movement) or verbal (spoken) and comes in a variety of forms but usually includes movements such as head nods, finger pointing, and shoulder shrugs while the verbal includes words like "uhhumm," "yup, yup, yeah," or "definitely." While these are intended and expressed by Americans as a way of confirming engagement with the conversation, filling small gaps, and expressing agreement, interest or sympathy, I've found they often confuse non-native speakers who see them either as an interruption, inquiry, or dismissive attempt to speed the person up.

Interruptions

Because we don't employ nearly the same type of strictly turn-based conversation flow, as soon as there's a brief pause it is viewed as an opening for a response. While this can be a challenge even among native speakers, it is a much larger issue when speaking with Nordics who often feel interrupted, ignored, or talked over.

This is where the two conversational styles clash the most dramatically as the Nordic is often pausing to collect their thoughts, breathe, and then continue their point at what feels like a comfortably rapid pace with the expectation that their conversational partner will similarly understand that they're still expressing their whole thought before advancing the conversation.

For Americans, particularly if they're highly engaged in a conversation, they'll endeavor to keep it moving at a fast pace in a rush to share ideas and thoughts. This means that anything more than the briefest pause to breathe will be viewed as either an opportunity or outright invitation to speak with longer gaps viewed as uncomfortable pauses. There is also a difficult to express set of rules for when you can interrupt for more clarification, disagreement, or to add details. Which in turn sometimes leads to conversational processes that override these acceptable interruptions such as, "No, no, no, let me finish . . ." and other statements which, while still present, seem to be radically less common among Nordics.

Longer Sentences and Tangents

Nordics take pride in saying something simply and are famous for their directness. I think this is partially cultural, but also comes from the nature of the Nordic languages which are often highly contextual and descriptive but tend not to have the same depth and breadth of synonyms as English. The lack of a word for 'please' in Danish is one such example of this in action.

This Nordic directness, particularly in the workplace, can be quite shocking to Americans. Especially those from the south, midwest and western parts of the U.S. where politically correct politeness is taken to an extreme. The end result is that not only do native speakers opt for longer and more complex sentences than may be necessary or popular among their Nordic counterparts, we will also use these subconsciously to fill or outright avoid uncomfortable silences.

Where for a Nordic speaker a simple "yes" might do, you'll find ample situations where Americans deliver a long explanation or carefully framed answer. This fills the space, gives them time to think and also allows for segues to other topics without a full conversational stop, silence, and then pivot.

Perceived Unhappiness

The Nordic inclination towards increased levels of silence and more complete but less common responses can lead to perceptions of unhappiness, boredom, and discontent. Since these attributes are often associated with conversational discomfort or disengagement among Americans, it is entirely possible for a fully engaged Dane to come across as upset or disconnected from the conversation. Which in turn tends to leave Americans feeling inclined to fill any silences that exist, change topics, or ask outright what's wrong—often to the complete confusion of the Nordic in question.

We'll Help

Out of our aversion to silence or a percieved disruption to the conversational flow and pacing, when another individual (Dane, Nordic or American) is struggling with recalling a word or over a word's pronunciation, it is common practice among many Americans to jump in and provide that word. This is in part an extension of the affirmation behavior I mentioned earlier—showing we're paying attention and invested in the conversation—as much as it has to do with preventing an uncomfortable silence.

However, to non-native speakers, it can also come across as disrespectful by being seen as a reminder of the individual's lack of native fluency or linguistic/conversational competence. It's important to note that this 'helpful behavior' is something that native speakers do with each other all the time. They offer it as an act of general politeness, not from a position of judgment or superiority.

It's Not a Perfect Science

While I've drawn these insights primarily from my time spent here in Denmark engaged in conversations with Danes, they're based on more widespread trends which can be traced throughout the Nordics. I think many of these behavioral and conversational characteristics are also relevant when considering conversations with other non-native speakers from other cultures and regions globally.

While I've couched it from an American/Nordic perspective for this chapter, bear in mind that you can also use these two different styles to become more sensitive to differences in regional conversational styles and even personality types. Beyond understanding how a culture or individual communicates and being aware of how that impacts how we express ourselves and act as a responsive audience, it also offers insights into other surprising areas.

For example, Twitter has always struggled to find adoption across the Nordics while LinkedIn and Facebook have seen widespread use. The difference? Twitter's 140 character approach is structurally aligned with American's rapid fire, fragmented approach. For a Nordic communicator, it's deeply frustrating as it lacks the ability to offer a more complete and fleshed out thought. Similar social media channels like Facebook or LinkedIn on the other hand, provide robust opportunities to create crafted statements in a turn-based environment. By understanding the process of how we communicate, we are much better situated to be more effective and avoid unexpected complications and barriers.

Social Discomfort

A couple of years ago I had a realization. As I sat with several friends, on multiple occasions, we'd arrive in a situation where they were uncomfortable. Before long, they'd get antsy, and comments would start to flow. Often it was about the people present or aspects of the venue. Perhaps the people were too young, or too naive, or acting too embarrassingly American (in several instances it was young college students on their first exchange). In other situations, the beer was too warm, or the venue had failed in some utterly trivial and minor but nevertheless comment-worthy way. Visualize the hipster that ends up in a trendy club and is utterly out of place or the polished model who regularly is at ease and comfortable in fancy cocktail bars ending up in a grungy little bodega that only serves beer and bitters.

In these instances, their comments were often somewhat embarrassing, in no small part because they're typically made fairly loudly or at the expense of those nearby. That sense of surprise though also got me to monitor my own behavior and, sure enough, I started to discover I had the same coping strategy. I also suspect it's a mechanism that is particularly prevalent in academics as it's often the easiest and safest defense to alleviate discomfort. In these instances, the academic retreats to their space of comfort and control—academic topics where they have mastery and experience shaping the narrative.

Ultimately though, it's also something all of us do and on a fairly regular basis. Those that are best at conquering the impulse are those that also seem to be exceptional at integrating into foreign cultures such as the photographer who magically connects with locals or the social butterfly that drifts effortlessly from group to group.

As I reflected on the impulse, I became even more aware of when friends engaged it and when I started to reach for it. In many ways, it's an extension of our fight or flight response. We differentiate ourselves from those around, based on our discomfort, as a social justification for leaving or for engaging in some mild conflict which in turn allows for our departure. In a complex social society where simply departing or casually integrating is rarely a purely unencumbered and simple action, it is an unfortunately resilient tool we are apt to fall back on.

Which is not to say that sometimes these complaints are less from discomfort and more genuinely from dislike or casual observation. If I were to somehow end up at a party, only to realize that it was in actuality largely populated by racist neo-Nazis, disdainful commentary and a desire to relocate as promptly as possible would be completely justified. And yet, even there, such commentary might lead to missed opportunities to learn—though only through brief and limited conversation.

One of the life lessons travel has taught me is the value and power of accepting people in whatever context they exist, and then working to converse and engage with them at that level. It may not be at a level I find overly intellectually stimulating. They may not be people I otherwise respect. But, in even these most disparate of situations, there are often unusual gems which you can learn from and walk away with. There are opportunities to accept the context of the situation and to learn about what is important to that person.

Or alternatively, to let your sense of discomfort float, swallow your pride, and then engage in whatever the activity or venue is that has left you uncomfortable. Are you grossly out of place at a wine tasting? Stick it out, perhaps confess your ignorance, and seek to connect with the people around you instead of building walls and sending signals that create barriers. The same upon arrival in a dingy dive bar. Trade in your fancy cocktail for the low-quality beer on special, squeeze into a crowded booth and embrace the chaos, grunge, and simple charm of the moment. Ultimately you are the factor that decides if its a positive or negative experience and if you enjoy yourself or make yourself miserable. You, and only you.

When we do this, all along the spectrum, we avoid doing unnecessary harm to those around us who are either happily going about their own business, or who have opened up elements of their lives to us. We also push ourselves to expand our boundaries in a positive way.

When I do this, time and time again, I learn amazing new skills, meet new people with fascinating stories, gain insights otherwise impossible to reach, and often have a damn good time realizing how badly my defensive attempts at compensation led me to misjudge the situation. So what if I find myself in a college bar surrounded by freshly arrived, utterly naive, and somewhat obnoxious drunken international students? I'll work to remind myself that perhaps that was me back in 2004 when I first came abroad. I'll work to smile, to engage, not to grandpa them, or to make snide comments. Instead, I'll work to recapture some of that naivete, to embrace the moment and to rekindle some of it in myself.

It is so, so, fundamentally easy for us to ruin moment after moment in our lives. We are constantly in control of how we experience life, the way we shape how events transpire, and whether we enjoy ourselves or not. So, instead of choosing to be uncomfortable, fearful, or aloof, often with little-to-no actual foundation, choose to embrace and immerse yourself in the moment. Accept that the trivial annoyances you've likely fallen back on as your defense mechanism are just that, and ultimately likely to reflect far more poorly on you than on whatever has you feeling uncertain.

Of course, this only works if you set boundaries and you know where yours are. There are times where disdain, dislike, or aloofness are justified. These, in particular, are when the situation brushes up against our boundaries or our ethics. While some boundaries are fantastic to push and expand, others are more fundamental to who we are and tied to our ethics—something that should always be uncompromising and have the final say. But, to properly be able to use these as a litmus test, it's important to clear away the coping mechanisms that otherwise obscure and limit us.

So now that a few years have passed, that I'm aware of this challenge and have actively worked to overcome it, how am I doing? Better. I wish I could say I'd abolished the behavior completely. The reality is, it's still there and in instances where I'm far outside my comfort zone or mirroring the rest of the group I'm attached to, I will, at times, revert. It's only human nature, and yet, I notice it when it happens and I am acutely annoyed by it. Not only because of my own personal failing to overcome it but because I know that I'm very likely doing unnecessary harm to those around me, shortchanging myself, and missing out on rich experiences.

All of this eventually boils down to that age-old adage *be in the moment.*

Dance is an Essential Business Tool

It was the start of my sophomore year of college. I'd just returned from Europe and was open to trying new things and conquering my fears. I'd always aspired to the ideal of the classical Renaissance man and felt the need to learn how to dance, but was afraid of looking like a fool. In a bolder moment, I signed up for a Ballroom/Latin/Swing hybrid class. Though I didn't know it at the time, I had just made one of the most important business and social decisions of my life.

Where at the time I saw dance as a one-off skill to gain and perfect—a hole in my path towards adulthood—I've come to see it as so much more. Some of the perks are more self-evident: great physical exercise, it's social, and it can be a wonderful gateway to meeting new people for romantic and platonic purposes. But, beyond that, there are added benefits that are rarely talked about. In this section, I'll run through some of these and I encourage you to keep an open mind.

Since I started in the fall of 2004 dance has become much more mainstream. The demographics in dance classes have changed and the anxiety and fear about being categorized as overly effeminate among men has diminished. The ratio of men to women in latin, swing and tango classes has equalized as a result. However, it remains something that is, at least for most younger generations, still quite intimidating. At the heart of where that intimidation comes from, is also an insight into why it's such a powerful learning space for our professional and personal identities.

It's no secret that for the average individual public speaking is terrifying. After all, it flies in the face of our primal pack mentality. The last thing we want is to be the lone antelope separated from the herd. It's like buttering ourselves up, adding salt, and then slapping on an *Eat Me* sign for a pack of wolves. It's also not a shock for me to say that being a successful, well-connected, and competent business person requires the ability to socialize and be comfortable in social settings.

American universities are well recognized for their emphasis on public speaking and the added training they deliver. Many programs include public speaking classes supplemented by clubs like the Toastmasters. Not to mention the entire literary genre on how to give speeches and present yourself.

While these all have merit, none of them are fun or, for that matter, all that efficient. Classes don't provide for any significant amount of practice, speech clubs are great but can be intimidating and hard work, and books take time and may tell you what to do but still don't provide a satisfactory channel or support network to do it in. Cue the dramatic music, flashing lights, and let's take to the dance floor!

At its very core, ballroom dancing—and I use this term inclusively here of all partner dances that also have a social component, but particularly swing and salsa—is all about relationships and presentation.

While it might be possible, it's pretty difficult to waltz or salsa without a partner. In addition, ballroom dancing has been used as the primary social mixer at formal social events for hundreds, and in modified forms quite likely for thousands of years. This all makes dance a must for the aspiring business professional and a surprisingly rich opportunity for self-discovery and development.

Physical Presence

Your posture and presence say a lot about you. Dance is beneficial in two key ways. It will improve your posture by changing the way you stand, look, and move while developing key muscles during the partner component of each dance. It will simultaneously change how you move by increasing your balance and physical presence while making you more aware of how your body looks and moves through space. A strong handshake is good but ultimately worthless if you lack the presence to back it up and the body language to speak clearly with your body long before you say a word or raise your hand in greeting.

The First 30 Seconds

In most situations, people decide a lot about you in the first 30 seconds. This is unfortunate because the first 30 seconds is also typically when we are at our worst and most insecure. Social dance classes and dance clubs provide the opportunity for individuals to interact with a large number of friendly faces in a relatively short time. This increases your comfort and first contact competency in general—not just when meeting or talking to potential dance partners. In business and startups, often a heavy focus is placed on what your elevator pitch will be. The same goes for job seekers, conference attendees or individuals as they navigate the complexities of modern dating. The amicable and open nature of social dance evenings delivers the opportunity to perfect and refine those first thirty-second impressions in a low-stakes setting.

The Confidence to Approach

It's incredibly difficult to approach someone you are not familiar with and then to try and strike up a conversation regardless of the audience or location. But, social dancing revolves around just this type of behavior. Every time you approach an individual for a dance or are approached you are building your competency and confidence. The added bonus is that in a dance environment most people actively want to be approached. There is nothing like positive reinforcement to build competence, and while the risk of occasional rejection remains, if you approach with sincerity and attentiveness it'll be a rarity, not a rule.

Be the Flame, not the Moth

Most formal events typically have several standard components: a nice meal, a live band or a DJ and a space set aside to serve as a dance floor. It doesn't matter if it's your favorite night club or a black tie event, the same rules apply. The dance floor will stay empty until one or two individuals break the ice. By the time a few individuals and/or couples take the floor a wave of people will follow.

But, who gets noticed? The icebreakers. Further, consider the message those early dancers send by not only taking the dance floor when everyone else was afraid to but by actually knowing what they're doing. In most cases, you'll have instantly differentiated yourself and created the perfect entry point for conversation for the remainder of the evening.

Wonderfully, traditional dances like swing and salsa are a cross-generational and cross-gender topic. There are few other topics that match dance for the breadth and width of people who find it interesting and a relevant point of discussion. With dance, not only do you distinguish yourself, but you gain a rare opportunity to exhibit confidence and culture— something that in any other situation would take a lot of work and be difficult to do.

Dance is Always a Relevant Topic

While you might find the occasional exception, and as with any topic you can be overzealous and overdo it, it's been my experience that almost all adults fall into one of three categories: they know how to dance, they love watching dance, or they have always wanted to learn how to dance.

For that reason, dance can serve as an incredible fallback/icebreaker in almost any situation. It's a magical topic that can be used to build familiarity and add uniqueness in the awkward early stage conversations that would otherwise fall back on boring narratives such as where did you study, where do you work, etc.

Dance also has an unusual set of characteristics that allow it to be tailored as a topic to suit the needs and interests of the audience. If you're engaged in a conversation with someone passionate about sports and physical considerations it is every bit as relevant as other topics and profiles. The history of a particular dance is of interest to the historian, the geographic origins or musical roots for the traveler or musician, and the cultural impact or romantic implications are all examples of how the topic of dance is versatile and has a compelling richness perfect for driving conversation.

Social Network

Life is about meeting people. Any successful socialite or business person is constantly looking for ways to meet the right type of people. Unlike bars, clubs, and other similar social settings, dance is all about meeting and interacting in a friendly and conversational setting. When you're at a dance event, it's about dancing and having fun first and foremost.

As a result, it's actually much easier to meet business contacts or make valuable social connections because people typically don't have their guard up. Now, make no mistakes, I'm not suggesting you go and push business cards or try and set up business meetings. But, dance is a wonderful place to meet people and to get to know them, to interact, and to expand your social circle. The dance scene also tends to attract people from more affluent backgrounds and with above average disposable income.

Just remember, above all else, when it comes to dancing being the best isn't about skill. It's about enjoying and enriching yourself, meeting people, and learning.

The Power of Carefully Crafted Examples

I distinctly remember a time sitting on a houseboat on Lake Powell and noticing Dad was smoking a cigar. The occurrence was rare, but not unheard of. I must have been nine or ten and he must have seen me watching him smoke. Instead of ignoring me or telling me not to do what he did, he asked me if I wanted to try it.

How could I pass up the opportunity to be like Dad? So, I remember taking the half-smoked cigar with, what I imagine, was childish flourish mimicked from the movies. That's right about when he told me what to do—take a deep inhale through my mouth, and then hold it as long as I could before exhaling.

For those with some experience with cigars, in general, you don't inhale, and never inhale deeply holding it in for an extended period of time. The result was an explosive cough that left my throat coarse, my eyes burning, my nostrils flared and my stomach queasy all while I dealt with the sour taste of cigar in my mouth reminding me of my folly well into the following day. It was all made that much worse by the fact that we were on a boat which did little to ease my discomfort.

At that moment as I handed the cigar back I think

two things registered for me. One, a fresh level of respect for Dad who I was now convinced was effectively able to sit and eat fire and ashes and enjoy it. The other, and far more important of the two, was a burning lack of desire to try smoking anything else for the remainder of my teens.

In that moment he had eliminated all of the mystique, all of the curiosity, all of the attraction of the cigar and turned it into scattered ash. In the following years as I entered high school and opportunities arose to smoke I never felt the urge and outwardly scoffed at more than a few classmates. I'd been there. I'd tried that. Lesson learned.

Of course, it could have backfired, and looking back on it I know he took great care to make sure it was unpleasant but not dangerous. Still, it stands out as a wonderfully effective life lesson learned without pomp or special context that made it somehow seem less genuine and which eliminated the sense of rebellion.

When it came to alcohol, however, the approach was a bit different. I spent most of my teens convinced both parents, but my Dad in particular, had a moderate alcohol allergy. In reality, this is to some limited effect true. But, it wasn't until my brother and I left for college that suddenly a transformation occurred and I realized the full extent of their commitment to setting a carefully crafted example for us.

Growing up there was some alcohol in the house, but usually just leftovers from BBQs or special gifts that sat collecting dust in the pantry. Thinking back, I can't recall any instances where I saw Mom and Dad drinking. I'm sure there were a few at BBQs or for special events or an occasional bottle of wine—but it was an extreme rarity.

It wasn't that they went out of their way to shield us from alcohol or people drinking at events. Rather, they were acutely aware of their power as role models who we looked to for guidance and insight on how to behave and charted a course based on that. What we saw were two individuals who might have a lone drink, but were never drunk. Who enjoyed meals without an accompanying drink. Who never made a big deal about alcohol and who treated the topic casually but were also careful in their phrasing. I suspect a lot of this came from my Dad's experiences running a country club for several years and regularly having to deal with drunks. We've also been inordinately lucky in that none of the family has shown a genetic inclination towards alcoholism which would automatically throw this all out the window.

But, ultimately, the moment that sticks out most was how it felt like a switch had been flipped once my brother and I had both started college. Suddenly, the house had a well-stocked tequila bar and the previous inhibition and absence of booze were replaced by a still moderate, but visible presence.

Now, as an adult, we can sit and enjoy a cigar and a nice Scotch together, and periodically we do as a wonderful way to connect and chat. But my path there was one that never tempted me with abuse or addiction and instead framed my way of relating to each potent aspect of our culture in a way that left me in control.

It was then that I realized just how consciously

Mom and Dad had worked to create a space for us that left a powerful subliminal impression. Beyond the individual examples, each approach has left a lasting impact on how I consider the lessons I set for those around me.

From Parent to Peer

I was blessed with well-rounded, intellectual parents that have a healthy relationship and invested heavily in how they crafted their lifestyle, how they allocated their time, and financially supported my brother and my endeavors.

They created opportunities that shaped who my brother and I became, exposing us to travel, history, culture and a constantly evolving list of experiences even when we made it miserable to do so. They have always been profoundly supportive. They also haven't shied away from creatively teaching us life lessons.

They worked diligently to make sure my brother and I had a healthy relationship; careful to avoid pitting us against each other and going out of their way to allow us to thrive in our own mutual spaces without competition. In many ways, the first phase of our relationship was relatively traditional. They treated us with respect but also infused us with a strong sense of responsibility. They were always available, heavily involved and supportive, but gave us room to explore and chart our own course.

At times they made decisions which I can only imagine were deeply difficult and came with risks such as relocating the family to a city with better schools, or pulling us from school for a year to travel Europe on a shoestring budget, and later for an additional year RVing around the United States in a 5th wheel trailer. In these moments they put everything on the line and dealt with our confusion, fear, and resistance, taking it all in stride. They were unapologetic about the decisions they made and in each case, with time, my brother and I came to relish the experiences that had initially been the most frightening and difficult.

When I think back to my childhood, one of the things that stands out in my mind is the seemingly supreme nature of their authority and the strong sense that one of the worst things I could do would be to disappoint them. Yet, even when their authority was at its most absolute, they went out of their way to draw my brother and me in, to co-opt us as part of the process and to engage us.

Later, as we entered high school and the early years of college, they were careful to push us to expose ourselves to new things, but never forced us to chase those beyond the boundaries of what we wanted. In the moment, where we'd have preferred nothing more than sitting at home playing video games, it seemed like they were being harsh or didn't understand us. Looking back, I realize the delicate balance they walked and the constant flow of new experiences they funneled my way.

Then, without fail, when we latched on to an idea or a hobby, they were there to listen. To nurture it. To support it. While an occasional hard "no" came up, far more often they'd ask us a series of questions, helping us gradually discover the unrealistic scope, or logistical barriers, or incomplete logic in the ill-advised undertakings we were considering.

All of this is to illustrate and express that they did a wonderful job being nurturing parents and fostering a parent/son relationship that gave us room to grow, to find ourselves, and to chart our own path. But, as college wound to a close and I sat on the precipice of adulthood our relationship faced a crossroads. By necessity, our dynamic needed to evolve to allow me to continue to find myself and to continue to grow as I further explored my own independence.

But, the path that evolution would take could have gone in a wide variety of directions. The most traditional of which would have intensified friction as we attempted to maintain the same dynamic, eventually leading to conflict. In other cases, my romantic partner might have swept in to replace key aspects of the role they provided with an opposing and nurturing voice. In others, our contact could have continued to fade, while the dynamic itself remained perpetually in a child/parent state, drawn upon largely only when I found myself in need. Others feel as though their role as a parent is largely complete and, just as they weaned the child initially, weaning the child into adulthood is equally necessary.

In our case, and the reason I'm including this section in the book, is that they did something that is wonderfully unusual. They fundamentally—and presumably very consciously—worked to change the way we interacted. Instead of speaking with pure authority, they approached our interactions with humility and carefully walked the line between parent, mentor, and peer. They made themselves available as a resource and collaborator on projects, without falling into a role where they dominated the project or pushed me aside.

They were always there to offer input and feedback, an evolution of the relationship that had already existed when I was younger. But, they were respectful of my choices when I came to different conclusions. Beyond that, they sought out my input and asked for my help. Each of these aspects created opportunities to collaborate. They also created situations where I came to trust their advice and rely on their support in essential ways as my editors, my confidants, friends, and mentors.

At the same time, it was necessary on my part to actively work to engage and reach out. Over time we created small rituals that enabled more regular communication. Perhaps chief among these were regular calls during my twenty-minute commute home from work to discuss the day, brainstorm on ideas for a potential startup I was considering, discuss my blog, and generally, reflect on everything from politics to economics.

That's where the dynamic truly began to change. I think this may be somewhat familiar to many daughter/mother combinations, but as a young man and someone generally averse to phone calls, it was a true eye opener. Our regular chats, sometimes almost every day, allowed us to weave a common tapestry of experience and reflections that were beyond a once-monthly summary call that life was "good" and I had a trip planned. It created a latticework upon which daily experiences were built and routines formed, but also which made it easier to discover and discuss topics of substance.

Within months, what had started as a call to brainstorm or get feedback on my new job and entrepreneurial projects evolved into a richer dynamic that transcended an individual period of uncertainty where I needed advice on a specific project. Now, almost a decade later, we continue our regular calls, despite time zone issues and six of those years spent living on the other side of the world from each other.

What began with discussions on economics, politics, travel and my projects has morphed into collaborations on a wide range of projects. These have included my Dad's ebook on education, the launch of his podcast, his blog and his voracious mastery of social media. With my Mom, we've collaborated on the promotion and distribution of her music, her own creative projects, and overlap between the spaces. Meanwhile, they are my primary editors, have served as sounding boards for my blog, my videos, photography, the launch of my podcast and navigating the professional challenges of first studying, then living, dating, and working in a foreign country.

Throughout it all, they seamlessly walk the line, at times treating me as a peer, at other times willing to cede the stage to my expertise and experience as it has evolved, and at other points re-assuming the mantle of mentor and parent. The opportunity to work together, to evolve our relationship and to strengthen our bonds has been invaluable. It has also created a rare opportunity for me to truly come to know both of them as individuals and to understand

and explore the richness of their identities beyond the role I saw them in as a child.

To that end, I encourage you all to step back and to consider where the opportunities are to open a dialogue with your parents or parental role models, if possible. Proactively seek out their interests, what engages them and then take the time to communicate regularly over a set period. It's perfectly ok to tell them you want to understand them better and learn who they are. Of course, in many cases, this is challenging or difficult due to the family dynamics, the ravages of time, or cases where parent and child end up feeling as though they're locked into competition with each other.

Ultimately though, if you can do it, you'll open up a window into better understanding who raised you, the life lessons that shaped them, who they became, and you can potentially gain new best friends deeply invested in who you become.

RELATIONSHIPS

A S I'VE NOW STOMPED past 30 and still find myself quite comfortably single, but ever so slightly increasingly inclined to look for a more serious partner, I find myself discussing love, relationships, and expectations regularly with friends. These musings come hand-in-hand with watching many friends engage in key parts of the cycle. Some are already transitioning into their second marriage. Others are having their long-term relationships implode either resulting in breakups or divorce, while yet others are engaged in deeply happy relationships and starting to raise their families. Oh—of course, then there are the other misfits like myself—still searching and enjoying the process.

Often the topic of finding the right fit comes up and my high expectations and selective approach to compromise is often a point of disagreement with friends. Ultimately, I've narrowed in on two basic questions that help clarify my needs, while better understanding how these differ (or align) with others. I think far too often we approach relationships with the assumption that they're all somewhat standardized and that our needs are marginally different but structurally the same. Something I find to be fundamentally inaccurate and misleading.

Do I Need a Companion or Do I Need a Partner?

This is a subtle difference. It's also a critical one. As I increasingly talk to more people, I've come to realize that while we might often speak about seeking a partner, what many people are comfortable looking for is a companion. The companion is someone who seeks information from you, who relies on you in fundamental ways, and who offers nurturing and validation in a more pronounced way. The power dynamic varies widely, but ultimately, it is usually fairly disproportionate. These are also the more traditional relationships we often see and, in no small part, what makes it so difficult for highly driven and successful women to find men willing to date them. This dynamic is often referenced as the student and the teacher or the provider and the nurturer.

The other approach is individuals seeking a partner. For me, this is essential and a fundamental requirement for a more serious relationship. While I'll casually date in a companion-style, I can almost always tell from the get-go that there is a disparity there—often tied to the spheres of a curiosity dynamic which I'll discuss in a moment. This fundamentally dooms any chance of it transitioning or being a more serious and committed relationship for me. The partner, versus the companion, is an individual that may have somewhat different interests and areas of focus or expertise, but who comes to the table in a more equal power distribution. This is an individual that offers some nurturing and validation, but who also brings a very heavy intellectual component to the relationship in the form of sourcing new knowledge, maintaining lively curiosity, holding opposing opinions, and harboring a strong internal drive that revolves around a give and take dynamic.

Interests and Spheres of Curiosity

Take a moment and think of your friends. Then make a mental list of their core interests. Tally them up. Then do the same for yourself. For many people there will be three or four interests: work, a passion project, friends, perhaps relationships, children, or their family if they have one. It's normal. They've also likely got one or two other key interests that may not be actively nurtured but which are somewhat present. When I make my list, I end up with more than thirteen. These are areas of passion and interest that I engage with at least once a week in some primary capacity or another. When I look at my network, many of my closest friends similarly have numerous spheres of curiosity—often double or triple the three or four that I find is most common.

This isn't relevant because one is superior to the other. It's not a question of intelligence, or of accomplishment. It's simply a way of better understanding where we place our priorities and choose to spend our time. It's a look at what we value as individuals and how we relate to the world around us. It is in indicator of compatability.

When it comes to dating, this has suddenly helped me better understand and convey why I'm often relatively uncompromising in my search for a long-term partner. I've learned that when I'm mismatched interest and curiosity-wise, the relationship will almost without fail be more companion than partner in nature. In the past this has created false positives for me when I found women who were incredibly intelligent, gifted, and driven, but who were also highly specialized and focused on three to five spheres of curiosity.

As I seek a partner, what I'm simultaneously seeking is a woman that is similarly scattered and eclectic in her interests. This suggests a woman that similarly harbors eleven, thirteen, or perhaps even more, core spheres of interest. Of these, at least half need to overlap with my own. From this plurality of interests and the diversity that comes with them, we gain a robust latticework upon which we can build a partnership where we can learn and be challenged by each other in a two-directional, balanced flow of ideas and experiences.

This is not to say that you can't have partnerships that share a more typical number of spheres of curiosity—I think they're quite common, especially with fields and people that are highly specialized. Similarly, while perhaps less common, it is absolutely also possible to have fantastic relationships where both individuals have a large spectrum of spheres of curiosity but still value and thrive in a companion-based relational dynamic.

And that, at the heart of it, is the key. I don't think one approach is any better than another. The important thing is to know your own personal preference and what you need. There is, however, a significant amount of cultural pressure that constantly pushes against the added diversity of a more complex match.

At the end of the day, I have also accepted that finding a woman that I have a strong physical and social chemistry with, who also shares a desire for a partner dynamic and harbors a wealth of interests and spheres of curiosity, is no simple task. Often, I've been told by friends—male and female alike—that it is unrealistic and that I'm being obstinate. But, I have time, and though other factors stand as obstacles, I've encountered women that meet many of my criteria, so I remain confident, optimistic, and comfortable as I continue my search.

Of late I've also come to realize why the two most common and dogged pieces of advice I've been given don't fit. These are either that I'm being unrealistic and must settle, or that my expectations are unreasonable and what I should really do is find a woman that has the potential to be what I'm seeking and then work to craft her into what I want. While I speak to both from a male perspective, I know female friends often face both of these messages but with significantly more explicit and direct feedback from their family, friends, and culture at large. I reject the first outright as utter tomfoolery. There's something to be said for the second at some limited level. However, only in a mutual and gradual evolution that is constructive while engaging with a true partner. It is not some strategic chess-strategy in which I assume the role of parent, teacher, or strategic manipulator attempting to control and shape another person to my desire and will. The truth here goes back to a common thread throughout this book—curiosity is a fundamental way of viewing and engaging with the world. It has wonderful rewards but also brings with it complications. One of which is often how best to convey our differing needs to people who have conflicting priorities, who may not share a burning curiosity, or a wide range of different spheres of interest.

A Different Way of Looking at It

To explain some of the complexities that go with truly understanding why both are ok, I want to step back from relationships for a moment and jump to the IQ scale. As a refresh, using Wechsler's 1997 classification, an IQ between 70–79 is flagged as borderline, an IQ of 90–109 is flagged as average, with a score above 130 being classified as very superior. Then also consider that there are very rare individuals who score above the 200 mark. For this mental exercise, I don't want you to think about the IQ scale in terms of intelligence, I want you to think about it in terms of complexity and fundamental perception of the world.

Now, consider that the difference between the individual with a 70 IQ and the individual with an average IQ of 100 is the same as the difference between an individual with an average IQ and the above average individual with the 130 IQ. Then evaluate both in terms of the brilliant individual with a 190 IQ or higher. Consider then, what it must be like for the individual with the brilliant or savant level IQ, attempting to interact with the rest of us on a daily basis. Even for the highly intelligent but non-genius levels of society, there is a larger gap in the ability to consume, archive, and draw connections between data than between what we would consider a highly intelligent individual and someone with special needs.

At this point, some of you are probably thinking back to the start of this section and wondering if I'm implying that those with relatively limited spheres of interest confine themselves to those of limited intelligence. I'm not. In fact, I'd argue that many of the individuals who are towards the more highly intelligent, but specialized side of things tend to prefer a more limited set of curiosity spheres.

But, what I do want you to consider is if you'd ever go to that savant or individual with an above average IQ and tell them that, not just for a day, not just for a week, but for the rest of their lives, they need to have an extended conversation with someone with a significantly lower IQ level. Would you then tell that individual, who still values those interactions but on a limited basis, that wanting to spend a majority of their time with someone better equipped to follow their line of thought and who sees the world through a similar set of tools, is unrealistic? Would you then tell them that their happiness required they settle?

In the case of relationships and spheres of interest, I want you to use this mental exercise in the context of the complexity of interests, not IQ. Consider on the one hand, a group of individuals that have a very narrow and specialized focus who are blissfully content with their one or two areas of interest. On the other, consider the individuals who thrive and need dozens of diverse interests. Now consider the potential disservice being done, going to those individuals with a sea of interests and shaming, lecturing, and pressuring them to essentially abandon or forgo having a partner with similar values and interests, just for the sake of convenience, pairing, and some semblance of partnership.

So, my message to you as readers is this: If you find yourself worried about the challenges you face in finding the right companion as an individual with a large number of interests and passions, don't be. There's nothing wrong with you. You're not being grossly unrealistic or abnormal. True, it makes it harder for you to find your right fit, but embrace and be unapologetic for your needs.

If, on the other hand, you're an individual who is on the opposite end of the spectrum, embrace and enjoy the richness and comfort you find in your own preferred relational dynamic. Seek aggressively to find the individuals who align well with *you* and give you maximum fulfillment in the specific areas most important to you. But also, work to catch yourself when your friend or potential partner has different needs and respect those differences. If you don't, you are harming that individual and demanding that they be something they are not.

Through it all, remember that love is not one-dimensional. Consider Sternberg's Triangular Theory of Love which envisions love, not as an absolute thing, but as a three-faceted triangle. Evaluate each relationship within the context of core components: intimacy, passion and commitment and then ask yourself how does this align with your needs and those of your potential partner? Be honest and in turn be happy.

Cheating, Respect, Jealousy, and Trust

Throughout my teens, I spent a lot of my time playing online video games. One of the big takeaways from that period was just how rapidly people changed their behaviors and how they justified those behaviors once they got online. From outright theft to flagrant abuse, the context of the game and the anonymity provided by the internet led many to dehumanize the interaction and to justify bad behavior. As soon as accountability and punishment were lifted, many treated it like a free for all.

Ultimately, this gave me a very clear insight into how some of us will act once anonymity or pseudo-anonymity is introduced. I understood it and, of course, at some subtle level, we are all guilty of it. But, what struck me most was how poisonous it was, not only for those individuals and those immediately around them, but the deeply negative waves it sent out through everyone they came into contact with.

So, in a way, I was already somewhat critically attentive when I first started to travel on my own. Travel provides a fascinating opportunity for self-discovery, independence, and the space to explore ourselves. But, much of that comes as a direct result of a period of increased independence and anonymity. For each of those positives, the part that left me shocked was how often relationally, people's behavior mirrored what I'd seen in gaming communities. Cheating or at least an inclination towards cheating suddenly became prolific, with a seemingly blatant disregard for the partner.

Ultimately, it wasn't confined to travel. It was just that travel, by more dramatically increasing the level of anonymity, illustrated people's fundamentally dishonest approach to their relationships. It wasn't the magic of the experience or the moment that made people toss their monogamous commitments to the wind, it was just the ease of doing it.

Over the last century, we've seen incredible changes in what's available to us as individuals. Automobiles gave us the ability to travel and rapidly relocate across vastly different geographic and social environments. Birth control gave us the ability to more easily have sex recreationally. The internet has given us access to new ways of connecting, including opportunities for romantic or sexual adventures. But, while each of these has made elements of cheating more readily available, history paints a pretty clear picture that it's always been an aspect of culture that was simultaneously strictly frowned upon but at the same time tolerated. The underlying logistics remain the same, it's just the semantics and terminology or tools that evolve.

But, my goal with this chapter isn't a moral lecture on cheating. Rather, if we're to operate and seek healthy and rewarding relationships, it is that we have to acknowledge the existing structure and suite of bad behaviors tied to cheating that exist. It's only from here that I believe we can truly pivot our focus to talk about the antidote to cheating—which isn't monogamy, it is respect.

Respect

When it comes to love, romance, and sex I've tried to live by a basic rule. Do no evil, and endeavor to leave the individual you spent time with in a better place than when you started. It's not always possible. Things go awry, mistakes happen, but at the end of the day it's allowed for significantly healthier interactions. At the heart of this approach is a basic focus on demanding respect from the other person and every bit as importantly giving them respect in return.

Which is to say, not viewing them as a resource to be tapped into, exploited, and used to suit my own needs regardless of the cost, but rather as a companion, as a partner, and someone to whom I have a responsibility. In this context, I don't cheat. Not only because I have a responsibility to the relationship I've established and the terms I've agreed upon with the person, but because more than that, I have a fundamental respect for them as an individual. To cheat would be to deeply violate that respect.

And that, at its heart, is the foundation of a healthy interaction and serves as a very powerful barometer for understanding the status and level of a relationship. If I'm ever tempted to violate that trust and the level of respect has slipped to the point where the allure of some exciting flirtation outweighs my sense of responsibility to that individual, it's time to abstain from temptation in the moment, and then go and have a difficult conversation.

At which time, that difficult conversation is one that has to focus on realigning with or changing the dynamics of the relationship with my partner. This is to say, fixing whatever the underlying challenge is that's diminished my respect or sense of responsibility to that individual, discussing a change in the dynamics of the relationship, or ending the relationship.

It's essential that we ask ourselves—do I want to be with this person? Do I want to be with this person exclusively? Do this person's needs align with mine and have we honestly discussed and confirmed that's the case? If the answer is yes, then respect and responsibility are well matched. If the answer is no, then you're fundamentally doing the other person a disservice, deceiving them, and poisoning the relationship as well as your ability to operate and live in a healthy fashion.

The reality is that while cheating most often focuses on sex, it's prevalent across the entirety of the relationship and is only one dimension of the overall nature in which you interact with your partner. If your relationship lacks respect, true, genuine, deep, respect for the other person—then no matter how many cute names you call each other, flowers you buy, or how sweet you are, it's not a healthy relationship.

It's also something that I believe is essential to shaping how you interact, not the context of the interaction. By that, I mean that one of the semantics I often see played with is a question of length or seriousness of the relationship. "We've only been dating a few weeks" or "It's not a problem, since I know he's not the one I'll marry" or even "We've been together so long it was inevitable." Essentially, justifying the disrespect and betrayal but implying it's expected or not an issue because the relationship itself is not serious or special is nonsense.

All of this in no way implies that it's not possible to have flexibility within your relationships. That respect and richness can be there in polyamorous relationships, it can be there in casual friends-with-benefits or fuck-buddy dynamics, it can even be there in asexual relationships where sex is absent, but other forms of emotional intimacy are paramount. The key is not just honesty, but honesty with empathy.

One of the other games that I often see played is pseudo-honesty. In these situations the individuals are transparent and they agree to the terms of their relationship. They disclose and agree what their expectations are and then they adhere to them. But, in it, there are times where the semantics of honesty trump acting with respect. More specifically, where individuals know that there's a power and interest disconnect and that their partner will agree to certain conditions out of desperation.

Despite empathically knowing that the partner isn't genuinely ok with something, or that it will cause them pain, they push for it, set an ultimatum, and get signoff. Technically, they've done everything they should have. But in practice, they've acted in a way they know will consistently harm their partner. True, they're being honest on the surface, but they're acting in a way guaranteed to do harm, poison the relationship, and at a certain level betray the other person.

Jealousy and Trust

We're hardwired to be jealous. The more we care and the more we have to lose, the more likely we are to also have to fight a fear of betrayal. Toss in the constantly shifting power dynamic in a relationship and it's an issue almost all of us struggle with and have to do self-work on. But, at the same time, excessive distrust, jealousy and temper tantrums have always fascinated and horrified me. People's ability to devolve into absurd tantrums, often that look like a chimpanzee throwing a hissy fit including chest thumping and throwing things, are commonplace and—minus their abusive, dangerous and childish nature—almost comical.

Yet, honest discussions and positive framing of what and why trust and jealousy are areas of relationships that we're so prone to neglect, are few and far between. Ultimately, healthy relationships are marked by controlled jealousy and trust. All of which is dependent in turn on respect for the key reasons we just covered. If you don't trust that your partner respects you and is able and going to act with your interests, feelings, and needs in mind, then the destructive response is to be jealous and not to trust them.

Similarly, even if your partner trusts you, if you're operating from a position where you lack respect for your partner and are acting poorly, you'll be prone to project your bad behaviors onto them, imagining the worst. Again, acting destructively and exhibiting jealousy and distrust. The result is abusive. It's fundamentally destructive, and it's a sign of severe relational issues that have not been addressed. Even if you're functionally dysfunctional in a long-lasting relationship, if excessive jealousy and/or distrust is a key part of it, then that relationship is fundamentally damaged, unhealthy and in need of immediate work.

Beyond that though, the games we play surrounding jealousy in the search for attention, positive affirmation, or related rewards are also insidious and harmful for the relationship. Centering yourself, operating from a position of balance and clarity, puts you in a place to not only dismiss but disarm those types of negative relational games when they pop up.

One of my favorite pieces of advice for mastering jealousy came via a sociology professor in college. He told a story of dating a highly attractive woman who was a fair amount younger than he was. One day, looking for a bit of attention, positive affirmation and to trigger a bit of jealousy, she casually mentioned that an attractive co-worker had asked her out on a date. The intent was, of course, not just to educate, but also to trigger jealousy and to gauge his reaction.

His response caught her off guard. Instead of anger, or an insult lobbed at him, or annoyance, he made a simple offer: Do you want to go on the date? If she did, he offered to pay for it. The response initially would strike most people as odd leading to second-guessing—was he being sincere? Did he want to break up with her? Was he being sarcastic? Was it a bad attempt at a threesome?

In practice, it was none of the above. His logic was simple. He only wanted to be with someone who wanted to be with him. If at any point, that changed, then rather than wasting time, heartache, or tricking her into staying with him, he wanted to know and for her to follow that other path. But, of course, should she choose that path, it naturally meant the end of their relationship. No cheating, no disrespect, no animosity. Was he a bit jealous? Of course. But mastering that jealousy and his ability to trust her, was far more important and constructive.

For me, this is the ideal embodiment of what we should all aspire to in a relationship which should shape how we seek to behave. It's imperative that we understand and master our own impulses. That we seek to act with respect and empathy and engage in our relationships in a way centered around trust and genuine desire to be present. In many ways, it requires much more from us, but it also opens up far more freedom, vividness in how we interact with people, and leaves us and those with whom our paths overlap in a much healthier place. The old adage states that love is war. As with most wars, I find this to mirror what happens when we stop talking and turn each other into assets to be owned.

Instead, why don't we all aspire to something greater? We own the power to transform love is war into something better —love is respect.

The Café Conundrum

A prolific frustration among many twenty and thirty-something women is their tendency to meet and date men who are ultimately untrustworthy, self-centered, and act in highly unflattering ways. In short? Assholes.

The most common explanations given range the gambit. Some draw on the psychology of flirtation and attraction. Others look to alpha-behavior. Yet others catalog the interactions as an indication of success or draw parallels to flashy mating displays such as those of male peacocks.

While all of these factors are in play, and without question, the location where you meet someone plays a strong role in shaping the dynamic—there's another essential factor that's largely overlooked.

Across most cultures women are taught to be relatively defensive and standoffish toward strangers. This is in part due to a constant onslaught of male attention, but also stems from a wide range of social norms, general supply and demand factors, and the typical complexities of dating.

From unwanted conversation in a café, to a deluge of unrequested dick pics on the internet, to painfully high levels of sexual harassment and sexual assault, most women are understandably resistant to being approached by strangers.

At the same time, many dates—particularly those which originate via random interactions at cafes, bars, the super market, or on the city's streets—inherently require being approached by a stranger. This also extends to the world of online dating. In online dating you're interfacing with people who are highly overt, proactive, and aggressive in their outreach alongside those that take a more measured approach or those that purely lurk. Some apps have tried to specifically disrupt elements of this process by forcing women to initiate, but adoption tends to be more limited even if the results are largely more positive.

For most singles in their twenties and thirties this social car wreck is how a large percentage of dates come into being. One individual is going about their business when another comes barreling into the midst of whatever that business might be, forcing an interaction. While that is, perhaps, a rather dire description of it. It does strike me that it is often a fitting depiction.

Unsurprisingly, this is also a period where women often face a daunting process of sorting through asshole after asshole, undermining their self-esteem while accompanied by a host of other dangers. The rise of self-described pickup artists or PUAs has only served to exacerbate the situation as they introduce added levels of manipulation, deception, and strategies for bypassing attempts at dismissal.

This creates an interesting landscape. You have men who are largely required to initiate conversation, facing off with socially uncomfortable situations, who are either blind to or have a vested interest in ignoring social signals and women who are well-practiced in sending signals that they don't want to be bothered and are disinterested. At a base level, this means that a lot of these interactions don't happen, aren't successful, or don't last long. But, it also means that the assertive and aggressive men who ignore the women's messages remain, while those most attuned to reading and being receptive to body language and conversational cues are respectful and disengage.

The telling part of these interactions is what it takes to actually overcome both barriers. Which, in many cases, is a relatively low level of empathy on the man's part. Consider, he not only has to overcome the fear of failure and social awkwardness of potential rejection, he also has to approach a woman who is very likely sending multiple signals she wants to be left alone. He further has to assume that, even if those signals are not overt, that if their roles were switched he'd want to be approached by a stranger completely interrupting what he was doing. Which assumes he's empathic enough to even put himself in the woman's shoes.

Then, despite the series of social cues of discomfort, or leave-me-alone she's communicating through body language, behavior, and perhaps even verbal cues—he has to persevere long enough to secure her personal information. As discussed elsewhere in this book, this often includes partially ignoring very overt and sometimes direct signals from women or relying on social niceties, politeness and the woman's desire for conflict avoidance to maintain his presence. In other cases this culminates in quasi-awkward situations where women give their contact information as much out of the hope of getting the man to leave and disengage as out of genuine interest or attraction.

Fast forward to a bit of witty banter, some exchanged text messages and a date or two. Presumably he manages to be charming, attractive, or at the very least dedicate enough complimentary attention toward the woman to flatter her. But, things sour and the woman is once again left wondering how and why she's ended up with another disrespectful asshole.

But, this is where we need to pause and ask, is it really a surprise?

In this instance, the type of guy that's going to come to the surface, be more visible, and most persuasive is most often going to be someone with extremely low levels of empathy and respect. In short? An asshole.

Of course, this doesn't mean that every guy that strikes up a conversation or approaches a woman at random fits that profile. It does, however, go a long way towards explaining why, time and time again, many women find themselves sitting across the table from someone who doesn't respect them, who regularly violates their barriers and who is unreliable, deceptive or untrustworthy.

What does this ultimately mean for individuals seeking healthy interactions? It means there are no good, clear, and clean alternatives. But, it also means that it's essential that we carefully examine our behavior and acknowledge that it doesn't take place in a vacuum. Every time we interact with a member of the opposite sex, we're existing as part of a greater interplay by individuals and culture which adds an oppressive level of context to how we interact. My encouragement to men is to act with respect, to seek to be the best individual you can, and to work to find ways to acknowledge and then positively alter the nature of these interactions. My advice for women is to be aware of how you're subconsciously vetting suitors and the very real impact that has on shaping who you end up with.

As with many observations throughout this book, this applies beyond the sphere of relationships. When you meet and interact with someone, regardless of whether it's tied to love, travel or business and when that person shows a fundamental lack of regard for the messages you're sending, show extra care and caution.

Ultimately, one of the best litmus tests for choosing the people you spend time with, is asking a simple question—"Does this individual seem like he/she has, can and will put themselves in my shoes?" if the answer is no, then it's time to get as far away as possible, as quickly as possible. You've found yourself in the company of a predator, and that predator will likely spin tales of gold if it gets them what they want.

The Inevitable Allure of Long-Distance Relationships

The longer we remain single and the more we expose ourselves to a life driven by curiosity, the more often we're faced with the challenging allure of long-distance relationships. Inevitably the path to them is complex and tailored to a specific set of unusual circumstances.

As a prolific traveler and later an international student turned sojourner, I find myself surrounded by the constant allure of long distance relationships and immersed in a peer group where long distance periods of separation are almost unavoidable. Some of the most spectacular women I've met were fellow travel bloggers. They were brilliant, they were worldly, they were profoundly curious. They were beautiful and they possessed the power to captivate me with stories and new areas of thought in highly unusual ways. Of course, that always came with a caveat. They were inherently also travelers, living location-independent lifestyles or based in some far off country.

It's impossible to know what opportunities I missed out on by refusing to consider long distance. But, over the years I've come to see opportunities like these as something far more complex and nuanced than a binary, all or nothing, situation. Being immersed at the front line in friend after friend's struggle with the same challenge has also given me an awkward insight into the long distance dilemma.

The primary takeaway? Long-distance relationships fail in the vast majority of cases. If I had to pull a number out of a hat, I'd place the figure as high as ninety percent. Cheating and some of the issues outlined tied to respect are key points of concern. But beyond that are deeper considerations which are often far more fatal to the success and longevity of the relationship. The long-distance relationships that seem to work fall into two categories. They are often either well-established and extend over a limited duration— 8 months or less apart—or they are long distance relationships that start remotely or out of a brief period (let's say a semester abroad or a couple that meets while traveling) and then within six to eight months relocate to be co-present.

Love, Is Love, Is Love?

Isn't love enough? This is the one question that keeps coming up over and over again. Shouldn't having a deep love for your partner be sufficient to transcend physical space, geographic boundaries, and the challenges of a long-distance relationship? After all, if it's true love, then everything in our cultural narrative tells us that it should be about our connection with each other on a deeper level. With this in mind, if we feel strongly for the person, if we feel the potential for love or, perhaps, have advanced in the relationship to the point where we feel love, then can't that be enough?

The answer in most cases seems to be yes. But only for a little while and only if we're honest about how we experience love and what we need from our relationships. Time and time again I find myself in long drawn out conversations with friends slowly going through the painful motions of ending a long distance relationship. It's rarely clean, and often the focus comes back to the fact that they care deeply for each other, that they love each other, only to go off on a long tirade about how insensitive or hurtful or inattentive the soon to be former partner is.

Which, makes total sense. There was, and likely still is, significant attraction. After all, there was enough from the get-go to risk long-distance to begin with. Add to that, the high-contrast nature of long-distance relationships where time together is defined by super intense fairytale bursts or hyper disappointing rendezvous that fail to deliver on the romantic charm and promise built up over the digital back and forth in-between. Ultimately, expectations disconnect from the ability or energy to deliver.

Binary Definitions Destroy Great Moments

In many instances "I love being with you" ends up being mistaken for, or automatically forced into becoming, "I love you." While the western view of relationships has evolved significantly in recent years, we're still driven by a semi all-or-nothing mentality. When we meet someone wonderful, we're pushed to either abandon that relationship or make it into something exclusive and concrete. This means that the man or woman you just met and found to be a wonderful companion, who is now returning home or has to relocate, becomes an all or nothing situation. Either you go your own way and abandon any type of relationship, or you lock things into a concrete declaration because you think there's more potential there. It neglects that there are many different types of love and that some last for a day, fully complete in that brief bubble of time. While others stretch across the reaches of time.

Unfortunately, just because you had a spectacular time discovering the Alhambra or enjoying a four-month exchange, doesn't mean that those rich experiences and that hyper-stimulated period will translate into relational compatibility. It's not unlike going on your honeymoon at the very start of the relationship and then assuming that the entire relationship is going to match that experience perfectly.

The realities of the relationship are what come when those layers are stripped away once the unique period of discovery and constant stimulation is replaced by repetition, responsibility, and routine. It's also even more complex than that, as the behaviors that are so exotic and exciting in the moment—that late night skinny dipping trip, or month spent exploring nightlife as an exchange student—are great for igniting attraction but bad for maintaining it.

As our level of investment in a partner advances, our expectations for how they engage with us, how they are loyal to us, and how they entertain themselves also evolve. Layer on long-distance and you rapidly face a sense of missing out or a current of jealousy or sense of disrespect as your partner continues to go about his/her life and partakes in a social life that largely excludes you even while you may be doing the same.

All of this means that in many cases, people fully expect the long distance relationship to fail. But, they find that because the experiences in the lead-up to that relationship were so magical or so special, that they feel an obligation to try and see if there's actually something more. Instead, more often than not, they come to associate those amazing experiences with the negative fallout and sense of wasted time that follows the eventual breakup.

This is by no means to say that it's not a brave and wonderful thing to have the courage to act on an opportunity when you do feel an incredible connection and more long-term potential. It's just to say that just because an experience or period is wonderful does not mean that it's the framework for a brilliant or healthy long-term relationship. I encourage those who do find themselves tempted, despite the challenges and obstacles, to embrace it. Just don't ruin something that could otherwise be wonderful on its own by being unrealistic about what it could become.

The Need for Co-Presence

Often, couples assume that as long as they manage a semi-regular schedule to meet in person, that it'll be sufficient to keep their relationship healthy. While this is absolutely an essential part of maintaining a long-distance relationship, it oversimplifies and glosses over many of the key underlying risks.

When you're only together for a weekend once a month, or a week every three months, you inherently end up falling into a distorted dynamic. The experience is either abnormally good, coloring expectations when you finally end up back together permanently or results in failed expectations where the hyper-inflated conversation and ease of expressing yourself digitally and remotely falls short when you're suddenly face-to-face once again.

Beyond this, the longer you spend apart, the harder it is to keep synchronized with each other's daily life experiences, and to align on the evolution of interests and shifting life priorities. Over time, even if all other aspects of the relationship are fantastic, simply by being apart from each other, you miss out on the micro conversations and daily events which propel us forward through our lives. A bit like two ships sitting on still water side-by-side, blown by the same wind—over time, subtle differences in the wind and the water will nudge the two in widely different directions.

This can be a profoundly challenging pitfall for many couples who, in all other areas, did and had something that was truly wonderful and worked. The love was there, the chemistry and alignment were there, but over time the difference in their life experiences during the period apart led them down a far less compatible path.

The longevity of many long-distance relationships is also often drawn out by the ease of coasting. If you were co-present, you'd face conflict, and that conflict or misalignment in needs would grow and be addressed more immediately. Long-distance creates a placeholder that leaves people committed and engaged, but only in a maintenance stage.

Often, after an extended period apart or the brief co-present period that started the relationship, followed by a long period as a long-distance relationship, the worst thing that can happen is that the two people find themselves living together. The fairytale collides with reality and a much less blissful reality rapidly sets in.

What Will You Give up for Love?

The other inevitable question couples must face is what they're willing to give up for the prospect of their long distance relationship. For the long-distance part of the relationship to end, there has to be a clearly defined path towards being co-present again. That working goal has to be set in good faith, with the expectation that it won't move, and that both partners are entirely dedicated to making the commitment.

Often, this means significant changes for one partner—leaving their home country, their existing social network, their job, you name it—all in the hopes of making a relationship work. That's not only a huge risk for the individual willing to make the leap, it's also a huge pressure on the other partner who often feels a significant obligation to say yes or is flushed with a sense of power and flattered by the interest, but eventually fearful of the implications.

In many cases, particularly when it comes to relationships that have evolved from travel or long-distance meetings, the couples constantly skirt the inevitable in an attempt to avoid confronting the logistical goblin hovering just out of reach. The focus narrows in on commitment, on vague promises or collective theoretical planning, but with no concrete path to making it work.

In other situations, the opposite is at hand, with one individual so eager to make it work or at a flexible point in their life that they'll relocate or dive in full steam without pausing to feel out and confirm that it's what the other person actually wants and is ready for.

It's Impossible to Engage Fully When You're Divided

While every couple that enters into a long-distance relationship does so with the aspiration that both partners will maintain healthy social lives and networks during the time apart, that's rarely the case. Over time, it becomes increasingly difficult to live in both worlds—that of the committed and respectful long distance relationship—and that of all other aspects of your daily local life.

If you anticipate relocating for the relationship, that gradual pull back from your existing local network is less of a fear. Unless, of course, the long distance relationship hits a turbulent period. At which point many find themselves facing twice the loss having gradually eroded and slipped out of their existing social network and routines and simultaneously are now looking at the loss of the long-distance relationship that had served as the replacement that gradually took over.

The gradual polarization of the relationship also creates other issues, as it likely happens more completely or more rapidly for one partner than for the other. The end result is a difficult lack of synchronization which triggers jealousy, self-doubt, and relational friction. Typically, the added statement of needs from one partner also leads the other, who then feels suffocated or scolded, to pull back further.

Sex Isn't Everything, But It Is Something

It's fairly self-evident that most of us are in relationships in part for sexual gratification. While we all have vastly different sex drives, it's important for couples experimenting with long-distance relationships to take a much more up-front and honest approach to discussing their needs and ensuring that they spend time together physically.

With the rise of Skype calls, video chat, sexting and everything else in between there are so many options to keep in touch in vivid and engaging ways that we often forget just how important it is to pause and have an honest conversation about sexual needs. If one partner has a more moderate sex drive or vivid imagination and can find sufficient stimulation remotely but the other has a high sex drive and/or need for more direct stimulation, the dynamics of the long-distance relationship have to take that into consideration.

A failure to do so inevitably leads to issues. At the same time, excessive digital intimacy with minimal in-person contact also creates a series of additional challenges in becoming reacquainted and drawing strong lines for understanding where playful fantasy from afar fits into in-person romance and sexual dynamics.

Power Defines the Breakup Cycle

Ultimately, in most cases, the relationship comes to a close. While sometimes both partners recognize it's unavoidable and are able to reach that point at relatively similar times and in an amicable way, oftentimes that's not the case.

Far more often one partner grows distant, fading away, trying to ease into a separation but this in turn causes the other to double down on communication and hold on tighter. Fights and a turbulent seesaw ensue. If there's excessive history, or cheating takes places, that often brings with it a significant amount of shock and pain.

As in all types of relationships, there's an underlying power equation between the partners which fluctuates with time. However, getting surprised by a breakup or news that your partner cheated, often blindsides the partner and unbalances that power dynamic. While true of all relationships, with long-distance relationships, the impact of having that power ripped away and the rug torn out from under you can be crushing. It also often triggers a deep sense of loss, even in cases where you already knew the relationship was wrapping up or were considering breaking it off yourself.

An essential part of the process is being prepared, cogent, and aware of your emotional responses throughout the process. This means working in a healthy way to preserve and re-establish some power. To be honest and realistic with yourself, acknowledge your feelings, protect yourself, and know that there is an unpredictable and highly emotional side of it which is very difficult to navigate. As you work to keep this all in mind, inevitably you can't help but experience a direct impact on the spontaneity and immediacy of your face-to-face relationship.

The Misleading Allure of Control

One of the most frustrating and yet invigorating aspects of face-to-face relationships is that not everything is within your control. As the relationship evolves and becomes more serious, you progressively lose control of things like how often and when you spend time with your partner. This isn't to say it's some negative or dangerous occurrence. Only, that as you move in together, or spend more time co-present, the relationship requires that you take a different approach to when, how, and where you interact with your partner.

The understandable, but taboo secret of a long-distance relationship, is that you're able to maintain much more control. You choose when you want to be available for conversation. You control where boundaries are set in a much more concrete fashion.

You also get to interact at a pace that suits your mood or needs in the moment.

This can be something small like waiting a minute to craft a carefully typed response. Or it can be more significant like delaying responding to/ignoring a message or setting specific times for sit-down dates. This also applies to in-person relationships, just at a much reduced level.

A long-distance relationship also gives you much more control over how the other person sees you. You're able to skip an evening if you are feeling ill or toss on a nice shirt before a video date. It also lets people see you when you're happy, or positive, or exciting and lets you obscure the less-perfect moments in-between.

For a truly rewarding relationship, these guards need to come down. Eventually, you need to embrace the flaws. Some couples manage that despite the added comfort long-distance provides, but most require time together, co-present, and in-person.

For many people, the added level of control and reduction in time you have to dedicate to the relationship can be a strong attraction to doing a long-distance relationship. It also creates a safe place to explore new aspects of yourself and how your partner responds without as much risk or fear of judgment. As with many of the dimensions outlined in this section, this added sense of control isn't good or bad. It's just something to be aware of and act on accordingly.

Placeholder Relationships

Perhaps one of the most horrible sounding types of

long-distance relational dynamics, placeholder relationships, can actually be (though rarely are) quite
healthy. Even though we've come a long way, there
are still ample reasons to find ourselves in a relationship that we know isn't right forever, but which is
decent enough for the time being. The key issue
with placeholder relationships is being fair and honest about it as well as knowing when it's time to call
it quits.

Unfortunately, they usually end up with a bad rap
because ultimately one person is in a convenient
holding pattern fully aware that the partnership isn't
right for the long term, while the other is falling in
love. But, a placeholder relationship can be perfect
for two busy people facing a variety of different social pressures or who just want a sense of intimacy
without pressure to conform.

With the pressure to find a partner from friends,
family, peers and even colleagues at work, sometimes
a comfortable and respectful long-distance placeholder relationship is the ideal solution. It's a mutual-
ly respectful and comfortable relationship that takes
the pressure off well-meaning but misguided peers,
and delivers an opportunity to chase your dreams, to
work on projects, and to have lots of time for yourself while still enjoying elements of the intimacy,
partnership, and periodic physicality that go with a
relationship.

Sadly, chances are far more likely that while one
person is benefiting from the attention, and added
support—the other has far more serious feelings or
expectations for the long-term potential of the relationship. Often this type of vampiric setup comes

about more out of convenience, insecurity and the difficulty in saying no or ending things, more than malicious intent. It is important to make intentions clear in the beginning.

Hope for Success

Having laid out all of the above which paints a fairly challenging picture—I do think that when people find a good potential partner and take the right steps they can make it work. I've seen some incredible relationships go through a long-distance stage and others start out in the most casual of ways and then evolve into a long-distance turned in-person relationship that really worked.

Moving beyond the confines of geographic limitations opens up a realm of potential partners which is far more diverse and flexible than confining your search to your own backyard. The ultimate trick is how to do it in a healthy way. I've seen incredible couples, who were forced to do long-distance over an extended period of time, slowly drift apart and nearly lose a rare and special relationship due to the distance and constant commute. Ultimately, what saved the relationships was prioritizing being co-present again and acknowledging, before it became too late, that a line in the sand had to be drawn. For others, it's a question of age, the maturity of your relationship, relational needs and knowing one's self.

At the end of the day, it also comes down to a careful exploration of what parts of the relationship and dynamic are most important for you. Understanding the allure and draw of the other person, what you'd be willing to do to head towards being co-present eventually, and having honest, clear conversations with yourself, and each other, is essential. I've included this section, and gone into significant detail, as I hope it serves not just as a framework and discussion about long-distance relationships, but also as a point of introspection for co-present relationships and existing partnerships. While distance brings certain relational dynamics out into the open, work, and even small distances between nearby towns can trigger many of these same considerations. Ultimately, how we would engage in a long-distance relationship tells us a lot about ourselves, our needs, and where we place our priorities.

Flirting and Ownership of Destructive Behaviors

For civilization to advance, it is of paramount importance that we move towards the elimination of sexism. A huge part of the onus for that sits with men who have a profound responsibility to educate, inform, and correct generations of tragic behavior. I tend to believe that what goes hand-in-hand with this is robust sex education and a generally reduced tolerance for tired and deeply damaging sexism. In life, and especially in dating, I like to ask myself one simple question—is the person I'm interacting with better, the same, or worse off after our interaction?

With this in mind, one of the areas I've grown increasingly concerned about in recent years is the hyper aggressive, deceitful, and destructive nature of a lot of what we've defined as acceptable flirting behavior. I've also come to realize recently that it also negatively impacts my dating behaviors and is one of the root sources of a lot of my frustrations.

In general, I've always taken a stricter than normal approach to romantic interactions. Yes, means yes. No means no. End of story. With rare exception, no doesn't mean try harder ... try again later ... try tomorrow ... wait ten minutes and try again.

The same often applies to the conversations I have had in the lead-up to different types of relationships. Yes means yes, casual means casual, exclusive means exclusive, etc. and with that comes a strong expectation that the individual wants to be there and if, at any point they don't, they leave. Respect and that level of commitment are fundamental, and it's why I also have such strong objections and disgust about infidelity and attention/cheating power games caused by deception and ambiguity.

Time and time again I run into two issues: 1) Women assume I'm not interested because after my initial expression of interest I haven't circled back and pressed more aggressively or repeatedly. There's some nuance here, but speaking in general terms, it's often the case. 2) Conversations and reflections on my relationships have demonstrated that oftentimes my partners assume that when we define or outline the context of a potential relationship, I'm not being completely transparent and stating my intentions. Rather, that I'm just feeding them a line, encouraging them to "win me" to "try harder" or that I'm just playing things cool.

And I get why they think that. Men regularly lie about their professions, about who they are, and about what they do when flirting at bars or parties. People lie about what country they're from, attempt to fake accents, pretend to be in relationships when they're not, or pretend to be single when they're in relationships. At a certain level, the primitive brutality and impish chest-pounding and assertive forcefulness are hardwired into us. From walrus seals to chimpanzees—it's part of our primal self.

Diving a bit deeper, this is why this matters and frustrates me and why the topic is an area where I want to see women take more responsibility. Particularly, I would love to see a pivot where women acknowledge their responsibility to approach relationships in an open and equitable manner. While it's flattering to be chased and there's nothing wrong with flirtation and playful banter, far too often across all cultures, but especially within many romance cultures, yes means yes and no...well....no means no sometimes, try harder other times, and yes but not now others. Which, quite frankly, is absolute bullshit and needs to change.

Why? Because it fosters and facilitates mixed signals, deception, and enables an abuse and rape culture.

When I raise this frustration, women often jump to justify it. Either highlighting that it's wonderful and flattering to be chased/a part of the game or that it's just ingrained in some of the cultures. To the first, tough shit, I don't care if you run down main street naked and pass out on a park bench, you should be safe from assault, and the simple onus is on men not to assault, rape or abuse.

But, at the same time, yes needs to mean yes and

no needs to mean no. This isn't to say that yes means complete surrender or commitment to the full range of sexual and relational aspects, but it should be discussed that yes means yes, with a caveat of conversation about where things stop and when they continue. I'm not saying yes means yes forever. Not at all. No, also doesn't have to be permanent, but once you've communicated that no? The onus falls on you to explicitly communicate the change.

As far as the second, cultural defense—tough shit. Having sexually predatory or rape-ish behavior as an ingrained part of your culture doesn't make it any more acceptable than stoning people to death for eloping or premarital contact. The consequences and emotional/physical damage are no less real. The risk is no less significant. The fact that there are cultural norms in place that accept and perpetuate that be- havior is tragic and should anger you to the point of wanting to take action, not cause you to jump to its defense.

Why does it matter? The issue with the lack of clear and open consent encourages ambiguity and it makes one of the most basic and fundamental aspects of the relational/sexual dynamic unclear. It's danger- ous, for all parties involved.

I can't tell you how often I've seen women com- plain about a guy, then later in the evening kiss him in response to his constant advances. When ques- tioned about the disparity it was often, "Just to make him go away." In other cases, the banter unfolds with an attempt of some sort. Then the usual cycle ensues. He presses. She says no. He doubles down with a why, or attempts to negotiate. She says no but remains. Fast forward twenty minutes and his persistence has paid off, they've left together, and he's just had all of those bad behaviors confirmed and re-affirmed.

This is, of course, reinforced by social norms. In the U.S. the pressure not to come across as 'too easy' and things like the 'third date rule' indoctrinate both genders from an early age to adhere to these approaches. But FFS, the world has changed, and it's time we do too.

Men and women alike can put as much pressure as we want on men to act with respect, but at the end of the day what many of those young men see is actions, and those actions speak far louder than words. The result? The result is that when that no actually means a hard, definitive no—I am not interested, do not touch me—then the two people are no longer speaking the same language. And if that no meant maybe, and that maybe can be twisted or forced into a yes . . . if the consistent advances and poor behavior pan out? The behavior is reinforced and rewarded which is exactly the opposite intention.

Or perhaps that no, intentionally meant maybe, and that maybe led to a yes, which could lead to a relationship. Then you've built the entire relationship on deception and dishonesty with your partner. There may be arguments here about uncertainty, but at the end of the day, both men and women need to own their decisions and take responsibility for communicating clearly. If someone isn't willing to do that, is that someone you really want to be involved with?

So, beyond the general issue with it endangering

women at large and fundamentally undermining efforts to reduce and aggressively persecute sexual assault, it also has frustrating implications for those of us who are committed to avoiding as much of that harmful ambiguity, deception and shady bullshit as possible. It makes actually finding, facilitating and initiating a respectful relationship that little bit more difficult and it simultaneously makes women distrustful of definitive statements by men.

My challenge for the women reading this who aren't already married is simple. Take ownership of the behavioral aspects you can control and work to evaluate and if need be, change your behaviors. The call to men is the same. Make no mistake, women definitely face more obstacles and social pressures in doing so, but it is essential to make yes mean yes, make no mean no, and flirt within the confines of those simple boundaries.

Travel is the Best Test for Relational Compatibility

For couples, particularly those relatively early in their relationship, travel creates an interesting opportunity to test compatibility. When we think of travel with a romantic partner, it's often imaginings straight from the movies: fairytale romance, vibrant foods, incredible nature, and constant inspiration for flirtatious adventures.

Of course, it's often a wonderful part of travel. The ability to share an experience with someone very special to you combined with the opportunity to craft powerful new memories that break free of your daily routines—it's intoxicating. Elsewhere, I speak to the power of opportunities that take us out of our regular habits. That holds every bit as true when it comes to relationships. Travel creates a very real opportunity to craft new experiences, to get to know each other better and to broaden the foundational memories that your relationship is built upon.

But, it also comes with certain risks and liabilities. Traveling with a romantic partner, particularly for more than a day or two, comes with a wide range of challenges and insights. These offer the ability to enrich and deepen your relationship and understanding of each other in new and exciting ways. But, they also quite often lead to revelations about the other individual which can be frustrating at best and shatter relationships at worst.

By its nature, traveling as a couple means you're virtually inseparable for the duration of the trip. It means that every small quirk and behavioral tick suddenly becomes visible. It means that the space you'd normally escape into, or the small oddities of an individual's daily routine are no longer glossed over or obscured, they're front and center.

It also means that we have the opportunity to see and explore our partner in different contexts—to see them under stress, to see them tired, to see them hungry, to see them feeling poorly. We learn how they navigate if they have a good sense of direction. We are exposed to how they deal with exotic foods or smells and if their personal hygiene aligns with the glorified version of dating. Through it all, we get to see how they react and deal with our own quirks. It's also a wonderful insight into interests. Perhaps they refuse to do anything but sun tan on the beach. Or, perhaps they're so caught up with chasing the next adventure they forget to pause and enjoy the moment.

There's also nothing quite as revealing and bond-inducing like realizing you've got a bad case of food poisoning, shit-puke included, halfway through a hike with no privacy, no toilet paper, and no opportunity for dignity. As traumatizing as experiences like these can be, they're also opportunities to see how the other person relates, if they're reliable, and how that chemistry aligns beyond what you'd have during a date, or a day or two spent together as the relationship got progressively more serious.

It's for that reason that one of the best ways to test partner compatibility, especially while early in the relationship, is a trip together. It's also why I'd never consider a relationship to be serious until I had spent at least a week traveling with a woman. Ultimately, the greatest insights come when we're co-present long enough to let our guard down and we start to show all aspects of our real selves.

TRAVEL

THE BEAUTY OF TRAVEL is that it is the very embodiment of curiosity fostered and unleashed. From the moment of mental inception, when the concept of a trip starts to take shape, to the nerve-wracking but wonderfully rewarding trip itself—travel is a profound exercise in self-enrichment and stimulation through discovery, curiosity and new experiences.

The ability to so easily transport ourselves far outside the confines of our daily world and the comfort that it offers is a captivating insight into the essence of human behavior. The absolute disruption of so many fundamental aspects of our lives, from when we eat to where we sleep, creates opportunities to test and explore ourselves in ways almost impossible in any other area of our routines. It also creates wonderful worldview clashes which reveal fundamentally different ways of thinking, relating, and doing things that we might otherwise never even realize exist or are within the realm of the possible.

Travel provides an opportunity for introspection and the chance to develop one's internal self confidence in a way that is difficult to tap into elsewhere. The combination of safety net in the form of tourist infrastructure combined with the exotic and novel nature of travel, particularly independent or solo travel, helps to strip away our daily support networks that tend to actually limit our growth.

Without these crutches in place, the path to discovering our true ability to succeed, overcome challenges, and master things on our own comes to the forefront. In this section you'll find observations drawn from these experiences, combined with travel across more than fifty countries situated on five continents and experienced through a wide range of travel styles that range the gamit from family travel to longterm life abroad as a sojourner.

Howdy: Cultural Identifiers and Their Value

Each time we interact with a stranger, there's a significant amount of uncertainty. When that inter-action occurs between people from different back-grounds, cultures, and languages, the level of unknown is magnified significantly. To convey our background and express ourselves while reducing that uncertainty we dress a certain way, talk a certain way, and when it comes to travel, we present ourselves a certain way.

Consider, why does the finance professional wear a suit and choose from a very specific set of haircuts while the tattoo artist opts for an edgy look that showcases creativity? What story do we choose to tell with our tattoos, our hair color, our matching—

or mismatched socks and the jacket we decide to wear on a crisp autumn evening? Each aspect of our appearance is a carefully, if subliminally, constructed series of signals we're communicating. Yet, when it comes to opening conversations with strangers, we're often far more hesitant to share these cues.

It's a common desire among travelers to fit in. This has significant advantages in the form of increased safety, added opportunity for cultural immersion, and the chance for increased experiential engagement. However, it also makes it significantly harder for you to communicate basic information about yourself to the strangers you have an active desire to communicate with.

While we will almost always be readily identifiable as an outsider to locals due to the brands we wear, the camera slung over our shoulder, or the day-backpack we've got strapped to our backs, it's not impossible to blend in with a little effort. At which point you'll notice your interactions begin to change, both with locals and other travelers. This can be great, but it can also create challenges and confusion.

So, where does '*Howdy*' come into all of this?

No matter how you've adapted to blending in or how hard you've worked to perfect the look of a local, the moment you open your mouth and utter a word people will know you're an outsider. Often, what they'll have trouble identifying is where you are from, and how to engage with you. Unless that is, you decide to help them. As an American from the Southwest, that's where the word *howdy* enters my equation.

With one word, I can share a wealth of information as I strike up a conversation. It tells them I'm probably from the U.S.A., that I'm a native English speaker, that I'm ok with a slightly more casual interaction, and that I'm likely friendly and open. One word used at the very onset of the conversation creates and establishes a baseline of common information upon which we can build a more comfortable interaction and a less awkward conversation.

To be clear, I'm not suggesting that you always use a cultural identifier, only that you consciously add one to your vocabulary and consider its value. As an American *howdy* is easy and differentiates me from other non-native English speakers, who use *hello* as well as other native English speaking cultures who also use *hello* but are not American. If I were Japanese, I'd probably opt for a big smile and *konnichiwa*, or if I was Italian the same but with *buongiorno*.

The catch? This flies in the face of all the advice you've probably previously been given about traveling abroad. That advice, almost without fail, suggests learning a few key words in the local language—hello, thank you, where is the toilet—you know the ones I mean.

All of which is great. But, it's ultimately a question of your goal. Do you want to empower and ease your communication with the person or do you want to attempt to engage them? While it's a lovely show of interest in the local culture, unless you're able to understand their response and engage in at least two to three exchanges afterward, all you've done is made your interaction significantly more complicated and created a barrier to communicating.

Examples

The first time I realized the benefit of using a cultural identifier like howdy, was during an off-season trip to the Greek island of Crete. I'd been on the road for 2+ months already and was apparently dressing more like a European than an American. When combined with my international facial features I could have been from almost anywhere. Time and time again in stores, or when interacting with street vendors, they would approach me and begin to work through a variety of languages.

Most started with German, then switched to French, then often Italian before eventually growing slightly frustrated and defaulting to English. These were individuals I wanted to communicate with, but with whom I was accidentally making communication significantly more difficult. The moment I started responding to their inquiry with an open and sincere smile, and a *howdy* we immediately began communicating more effectively.

Hostel common areas provide another excellent example. In these spaces, there's really only one well-grounded assumption to be made—that the people you're about to interact with could be from anywhere in the world. In these spaces, the level of social uncertainty is magnified. While almost everyone is eager to socialize there's a high level of uncertainty in the initial interaction. In these types of situations, everyone is hungry for any hint that helps them relate and connect with other people. Once again, this is a perfect chance to use a cultural identifier to help reduce anxiety and build common ground.

One of the most interesting situations is when the shoe ends up on the other foot, which in this case, is when locals or other foreigners approach you with questions. These instances can be somewhat awkward, as you may or may not have a decent familiarity with the area or subject they're asking about. They've approached you, a perfect stranger, with the assumption that you're probably local, and they have already taken a social "risk."

That risk they've taken? It's made more awkward if you don't understand their inquiry, or if you have to ask them to restate it. A process which can be accelerated, or avoided altogether with a word or two right off the bat. The added benefit is that words like *bonjour* and *howdy* can be spoken immediately, even if the other person has already started to talk, without being impolite.

Subtle Language Requests

To be fair, when you use a cultural identifier like *howdy* you're doing more than just expressing information about yourself. You're also subtly inviting the other person to have the conversation in your native language.

If you'd prefer to try and remain in the other person's native language, it may be worth considering what regional salute is suited to that language, or opening with your own cultural identifier and then adding a brief phrase in the local language. This tells them your native language, but then also indicates that you're interested in continuing in their language.

The Stupid Travel Myths We Believe

When it comes to travel, there are underlying narratives that insidiously discourage us from exploring wonderful opportunities. I always get annoyed when people tell me they can't travel because it's unsafe (my chances of getting robbed, stabbed, shot, or killed were far worse in Arizona than wandering Europe). Even many of the governmental announcements we've seen in recent years ignore context and roll out absurd statements that do little more than invoke fear.

But, the real truth I've come face-to-face with over the past couple of years is that I buy into my own version of this nonsense. The part that really pisses me off about the whole thing is that it keeps me from embracing amazing experiences, makes me standoffish, much more conservative in my approach when I start, and adds bucketloads of anxiety.

One of my greatest wake-up calls came when I finally visited Asia. For more than a decade I had avoided it, down-prioritized it, and bought into a number of different narratives which discouraged me from visiting. Most of you no doubt have a region (or regions) where you feel your own mixture of similar concerns. In this section, I'll use examples tailored specifically to Southeast Asia (S.E.A.), but I want you to ask yourself how these might apply to your own story and perspective.

My Matrix of Fears

Fear

Simply put, the Asia I had built in my mind was a very alien place where getting around using English would be difficult, where everything would be deeply exotic, and where even the most basic of daily activities would be challenging. Add to that a fear that I'd encounter large amounts of human and animal suffering led to a very mixed emotional response to visiting the region.

Lack of Interest

When I was younger, I had a very strong interest in Greco-Roman and Medieval history. That naturally drew me to Europe. The areas we're most interested in varies from person to person, but inevitably there are regions that have a stronger draw for us than others. Identifying what those are is something we rarely do overtly, but can be wonderfully illuminative in deciding where to chart our trips.

In my case, while there were elements of ancient history in other regions that sparked passing interest, none had the raw allure of Europe. In truth, I felt Asian history was somewhat uninteresting. I was not enamored from a cultural perspective and had only minimal interest in more recent cultural creations (e.g. Anime or food). As I've traveled more, learned more history, been exposed to more culture, and pivoted more to an interest in food, much of this has changed. Asia has increasingly grown in appeal. It's cliché to reference a flower blooming, but I often feel that's the most accurate way to imagine my interest in regions like S.E.A. and the entirety of Africa.

Cost

This is an odd one, as S.E.A. has always been extremely popular explicitly because of its relatively low-cost areas. It's why regions such as Vietnam and Thailand are thick with travel bloggers and has been a major tourist draw for decades. But, the flights from the U.S. and Europe were usually fairly high which immediately ruled S.E.A. out. I don't think the pricing itself was the primary factor, but when combined with my other areas of resistance, it served as the perfect justification to choose an alternate destination.

Novelty

This is a tricky one to convey. I've long felt strongly that it is important to act on opportunities, to embrace the moment, and to immerse yourself in experiences fully. I'm also a firm believer that both the destination and our own personal way of experiencing the world are constantly evolving. The end result is that a visit to Paris as a novice traveler will differ greatly from your experience as an experienced traveler. You will never see or experience a place the same way as you would have if you went now and the more we travel and are exposed to, the more our relationship with novelty and new cultures evolves.

Globally, if we stereotype regional cultures down to geo-cultural macro-groups, there are regions that share some (albeit very limited) cultural characteristics. As my travels took me to different continents and exposed me to different cultures that were similar to where I had been, I felt a shred of sadness as the fear, novelty, excitement, and sense of pure discovery that came from exploring an entirely new region faded away.

As I got a taste of Europe, Central America, South America, the Middle East, and Africa, I felt as though the last great region to explore and discover became Asia with the potential extension to include a separate Eastern Eurasia and India. While I still have an enormous amount of exploration, discovery and novel cultural exploration to do in all of these areas, I found myself keeping Asia to the side as one of my quasi-last opportunities for that utter sense of the unknown. In a way, it became the last slice of ribeye, set aside while I cleared the rest of my plate, waiting to enjoy it as a last delicious bite.

Myths

For years I'd been very resistant to a visit to S.E.A. and before that, large swaths of Africa because of different fear-based factors. Even though I ultimately found these to be greatly exaggerated, don't mistake this chapter as implying that some of these concerns aren't justified in rural (or other) areas and that they can't be present in traditional tourist areas. Rather, the takeaway from this section should be that they are far from the prevalent, unavoidable, and highly experientially potent experiences we've been led to believe. Instead, they're considerations, but rather minor ones.

Toilets

I'm lactose intolerant, have a sensitive stomach, tend to be a bit of a germaphobe, and generally have a thing about bathrooms. I'm also quite tall and quite inflexible with very tight Achilles tendons due to salsa/dance and wearing predominantly heeled boots which make squatting flat-footed impossible and any long-duration (more than fourty seconds) squatting extremely difficult and uncomfortable.

Based on discussions, topics, videos—you name it—my expectation was that nearly every bathroom in Asia outside of Japan's ultra modern robot-toilets were some variation on squat toilets. Descriptions of filthy hole in the ground squat toilets with shit-smeared walls, filthy water, and crud-encrusted sprayers were prolific and what I was expecting. This had been a similar fear about Africa, which had, to a lesser extent ended up being somewhat true. Though, there again, it was largely western-manufactured mythology or limited to very remote or poorest parts of the countries I visited.

Squat toilets are also a massive logistical pain in the ass, and I always find myself in perpetual fear that I'm going to spray my shoes, pants, and legs. In talking to most western travelers, many have similar fears which often lead them to completely strip naked before using squat toilets or perform some random mixture of bathroom-based acrobatics.

It's a bit childish perhaps to make a big deal out of this, but for me, it's a major factor. If I'll be hitting the toilet at least once a day, with the possibility of more while feeling rather unpleasant, that last thing I want layered on top of everything else is a miserable and embarrassing experience.

Then there was also the on-going confusion on just what the hell I was supposed to do with what. Was that big bucket full of water sitting next to the toilet for splashing your bum with? Or washing your poo-covered fingers? Weren't you then bum-water cross-contaminating yourself with every other filthy poo slinger who had visited the toilet before you? What about the hose, reminiscent of the one we use for dishes in the kitchen sink in the U.S.? Just how exactly was I supposed to use that without drenching myself or leaving the bathroom with a soaking wet bum? Also, hadn't every other filthy poo-fingered person who came before me grabbed that exact same handle, doused it in poo water, and then wandered off?

You can imagine my level of anxiety as my plane touched down in Vietnam, and the immediate sense of surprised relief when I discovered western toilets just about everywhere I went. Lots and lots of toilets. Normal, seated, western toilets. In fact, despite multiple visits to Asia, in total accounting for nearly forty-five days of total travel, I've never had to use a squat toilet. Of course, I saw a few, and if the timing had been a bit different, once or twice there's a small chance I might have had to use one. But, the reality is that even in non-tourist restaurants, homes, and destinations, the toilets were more often than not sitting toilets. Now, true, one or two lacked seats, but you'll find the same in the U.S. if you go to a dingy enough place.

I also finally got concrete explanations for what your basic methods and types of toilet protocol are. You have your conventional western toilet at one extreme. This can be used with paper that is flushed, or as is more common outside Europe and the U.S., a fold/twist and deposit in a covered wastebasket method. In many areas, you also have the hose I mentioned. This is where the whole clean right hand, dirty left hand comes into play. When sitting on the toilet, you sit as far back as possible on the seat, thread the sprayer in between your legs (some from the front, others from the back) and use the hose to spray upward. Depending on what you feel is needed this is all done with your right hand, and you can add your left hand, either from the front if there's room or back to gently aid the flow of the water. Once done, there's usually toilet paper on hand, but it's used to pat dry the water.

You'll also sometimes find a large bucket of water, though this is not to be used on your bottom. Instead, it's used to flush manually. If you look at how your traditional toilet works, flushing just floods and pushes old water up and over an air pocket then down into the pipes. We're used to having this stored and dumped from a large tank, but there's not necessarily any need for this. The pan/large water bucket is just a relocated water tank. When done, scoop water, and dump it in until you've replaced the polluted water in the toilet with clean water. These otherwise function like normal toilets and may be used with or without paper or a hose.

Then you have your squat toilets. A surprising number of Westerners come to love them. Frankly, I'd rather take a poop in the woods. The logistics of these merit added research, upon which the Internet offers a wealth of how-to advice.

Ordering and Food Poisoning

I've eaten some really odd street food, and through it all, have done quite well despite more than a month spent in various parts of Asia. This was in sharp contrast to the near constant, back-to-back food poisoning I was anticipating and expecting to mar the entirety of my trips. Overall, regardless of the destination, there might be a day or two with a mild stomach gurgle. But, pairing good practice with a strong probiotic has done wonders for ensuring any uproar is gone within an hour or two.

Finding food, even in remote areas, is almost always a simple experience as long as you relax, look around, and engage with the waiter. Throughout Asia almost every place I ate had some sort of English menu stashed away. These included small local places. As far as what I'd order—it varied based on my gut feeling for the area, how meat and fish seemed to be prepared, and what sort of refrigeration I anticipated was available.

Everything I had heard from people led me to believe I'd be getting sick almost instantly and was guaranteed to spend the next five days miserable in some dingy, bug-infested, bathroom hell-hole straight out of one of the *Saw* movies. While food poisoning is obviously a very present risk, and you're eating food you're definitely not familiar with or used to, the general level of hygiene when it came to food handling and maintenance was normally quite decent. There are always exceptions. One comical one that stands out involved an incident at a Cambodian street-side stand where a cat walked by with a massive rat as I ate, and where I found two small insects floating in my soup. But by and large, the food was fresh, clean, and delicious.

Of course, it's also important to protect yourself. On recent trips to Africa and Asia, I've started regularly taking daily probiotics, supplemented by a booster probiotic if something seems funky. But, the long and the short of it? Everything I'd been told and taught to expect about the food was misleading and overstated. The flavors, spices, and tastes that I found myself immersed in as I ate my way across Asia remain some of the most flavorful and memorable I've ever had.

This vastly different than expected experience left me reflecting on the common mistakes I watched tourist after tourist make. First, I suspect that most blame an upset stomach from the heavy drinking they're doing on bad food. Second, most people are extremely poor at identifying bad seafood. This isn't just an issue when traveling, as I'm always shocked by the seafood no-nos regularly on display in the U.S. and Europe. Simply by following traditional best practices for seafood, most travelers would easily reduce how often they get sick. My go-to steps are to check to see if the fish's eyes are clear. If they're cloudy, the fish is old. Shrimp and other seafood should not have a strong ammonia smell. If it does, it is old. Clams or oysters are usually best avoided, and should never be open before they're cooked.

Third, I'm always surprised how people assume that western food, ordered in a place where most people aren't eating it, is somehow assumed to be safe. It seems only obvious that the 'safe' hamburger or corn dog, is probably far more dangerous than the local meal of the day since it's likely served at a far lower frequency, has to be ordered from further away, is more expensive for them to handle, and much more likely to spoil.

Countries Awash in Danger

Every time I head to a country that I assume will be dangerous, I'm surprised by how different (safe) the reality is when compared to their reputation. Of course, I'm not going to take a visit to Honduras anytime soon or head to Syria in the midst of a war. But, for countries like most of those in Southeast Asia, places I often imagined being quite unsafe, I was stunned by how much safer I was than in most cities in Europe and the United States.

And, when I was doing something foolhardy, random locals usually chimed in to look out for me. On multiple occasions, completely random locals told me to be careful in Vietnam about how I was recording video from the back of a moped. Why? Because of a limited risk of snatch and grabs. Fair enough. That would apply equally in the U.S. or Italy.

I've also taken my full-sized DSLR camera with

me on each trip and used it in virtually all of the places I went. True, I was very careful with it and my phone (most of the time) and made sure to hold it securely, while paying special attention to my surroundings. I was also careful not to pull it out, or have it hanging on my side lazily in particularly dodgy areas. But, I often felt safer and less likely to get mugged in 'unsafe' parts of Asia than I do in Phoenix or London.

Often, the only real threat in many of these countries is conventional snatch and grab or pickpocketing. These are normal risks and should not be viewed as abnormal or blown out of proportion. More often than not, when I do encounter another traveler who has had issues arise, the culprit isn't a local, it's another tourist.

In general, the more I travel, the more I find that locals are almost always extremely friendly and proud to represent their home. If lost, or concerned, all I need to do is approach one or two locals, and in most places, you find they'll go out of their way to be extremely helpful and kind. It's always a humbling experience.

My travels in Southeast Asia and China also provided an opportunity to visit different regions and areas considered 'dangerous' such as Central Myanmar or Southern Thailand. In these cases, perception is drawn from more generic articles about the government and their politics, some minimal level of civil unrest, the alleged threat of terrorists targeting tourists or in other cases simply due to grossly inaccurate and offensive depictions based merely on large Muslim (or other minority) populations.

Short of actively antagonizing the groups involved and being reckless, these were all manufactured issues or grossly overstated risks perpetuated by western media and a headline-driven western narrative. The reality though? I was probably safer in these areas going about my daily business than I would have been during my daily commute at home. While heartbreaking and terrifying, I consider the real threat from terrorists to be negligible. Issues with government officials and civil unrest are, as usual, easily avoided if you're not being an idiot and don't decide to lecture the Communist Military Police officer sitting behind you about their governmental policies or hang around a political march. Civil protests are few, far between, and easily avoided. As far as the "Muslim" threat . . . this boils down to little more than absurd ignorance and racism.

In a period where terrorism and negative depictions of the world are becoming more and more violent, I think it's important to do your research. It's essential to understand how often these headlines are misleading and to act with intelligence, but from a position based on reality and context, not empty fear or myths.

Vendors are Pushy and Aggressive

I don't like pushy vendors. No one does. They're annoying, they're rude, and they leave you feeling uncomfortable. Based on some stories, films, and various western narratives I had been led to expect a lot of extremely aggressive, obnoxious and pushy vendors (and people in general). In practice, the only group I found this to be particularly true of was taxi and *tuk-tuk* drivers in Bangkok. Two groups which I'd be happy to see go bankrupt or punched in the face. Preferably simultaneously. But, I can also say that about taxi drivers in most countries, so I can't attribute that to Asia any more than Ljubljana.

Outside of this small subset, most vendors were very polite, relaxed, and anything but obnoxious. In truth, most were wonderful, friendly and extremely helpful. My experiences closely mirrored what I'd found when I visited Turkey, Italy, and Argentina. Large markets that are heavily touristy such as the Grand Bazaar (Istanbul) or the backpacker streets in Saigon and Bangkok tend to have pushy vendors. The aggressive and rude nonsense, however, is confined almost purely to these areas. Walk five minutes in any direction outside of these areas, and that rude intensity evaporates almost instantly.

The other part has to do with how you engage as a tourist. Your eye contact, hand motions, and statements convey your level of interest and engagement. I found quite often that even the most persistent of merchants in the most touristic parts of town were still easy to get rid of when I was polite, but firm and refused to engage.

I think it's also important to note that the locals in these regions are extremely friendly and helpful in general. Quite often many tourists are so afraid based on the negative experiences they've been told to expect, or one or two bad experiences with a 'friendly helpful local' who then agressively request a tip, that they miss out on the incredible hospitality and friendliness of locals. At the end of the day, keep in mind where you are and who the person is who has approached you.

Time and time again as I found in Turkey, Zanzibar, and elsewhere, the market and street merchant experience you see in most movies rarely pans out in reality. Especially if you move even slightly beyond the most touristed and manufactured shopping experiences.

Everyone is Trying to Con You

Based on everything I had heard, a major part of me expected to get home exhausted at the end of every day having spent the majority of my time fighting with people trying to take advantage of me. Obviously, as with pushy vendors, some caution is needed and a sense of situational awareness, but no matter where in the world I've traveled, by and large, the vast majority of my interactions with people were incredibly pleasant. In Asia in particular, most cultures have a profound dedication to hospitality, warmth, and social responsibility. As a foreigner, most locals will view you as their guest and be thrilled at the opportunity to talk to you, include you, and share with you.

More often than not locals went out of their way to help me, look after me, and to share with me rather than somehow trying to get something from me or con me. In short, the people were incredible and far more gift-giving, benevolent, inclusive, and eager to help me than I think you'd find almost anywhere in the West.

Is that *tuk-tuk* driver in Bangkok probably a

smarmy jackass? Yeah. But, then again, is that a surprise? And even there, for every schmuck I encountered, I met other folks like my *tuk-tuk* driver and guide in Cambodia who were warm, helpful, went out of their way to offer exceptional service, and were absolutely trustworthy while delivering great value.

So, if you feel like most of the people you're encountering are trying to take advantage of you, it's probably time to take a five-minute trip somewhere else. You're more than likely immersed in an area that is a grossly distorted version of the local community and population or sending out signals that explicitly attract the dregs of humanity.

Transportation

Getting around Southeast Asia was surprisingly easy. I was expecting miserable chicken buses completely over packed with smelly people while finding myself trapped for hours without restrooms or on ferries which threatened to sink at any moment.

Thanks to movies and online narratives I had a vision of Asia as this impenetrable warren of street signs and transportation systems that would leave me lost, confused, isolated and at risk.

Getting around, be it via regional buses or inside cities, was straight forward and cost-friendly. Add to that, the cheap price for a SIM with data, and the ability to track your location via GPS, and suddenly even the most daunting bus ride becomes straight forward. In truth, most horror stories from Southeast Asia likely result from one or two bad pockets. Chief among them? Bangkok's *tuk-tuk* drivers and their gasoline stamp/suit shop stop scams or the "metered" taxi drivers that won't make meter-based trips.

Even without a SIM, a cached version of the city with WiFi enabled + GPS tracking, is a great, if largely unnecessary, way to cross check where you are. Vehicles may be a bit run down and not the nicest, but in general are usually fully functional and decent.

One thing I loathe is long-duration bus trips. When it came to long-haul trips, I ultimately opted for several to save money. Some were up to 14 hours and included everything from buses to sleeper trains. In general, as deeply unpleasant as I found the long-haul runs, there was always still a functional restroom on board, the seats were clean, and the vehicles were in good shape. Some of the other long and mid-haul vehicles were super easy, clean, modern, and relatively spacious. For those where there wasn't a bathroom on board a quick shout to the driver inevitably led to a restroom stop within a few minutes— something that a number of locals took advantage of.

Language Barriers

Another common myth I run into is that virtually no one in S.E.A. speaks English and that it'll be difficult to navigate and get things done. While this might be a bit of a problem in the most rural of areas, or as you head out of S.E.A. and up towards China, and while it's true, there wasn't a profoundly high level of proficiency in many areas, locals spoke ample English to get by. Or, failing that, were always happy to track down a young kid or someone nearby who could translate if needed.

In many areas I didn't feel like the level of fluency was *that* much lower than parts of Central and Eastern Europe and in general follows a similar pattern—the young children speak a bit of English, folks my age are a toss-up, and the older generations tend towards much less fluency.

Even in instances where language barriers were present, the incredible warmth, friendliness, and hospitality-inclined nature of the locals in each of these countries made these language gaps largely irrelevant and they were never problematic.

Is That the Asia You've Been Taught to Expect?

So, have I learned my lesson? I sure hope so. Once again the myths that I'd been fed and consumed proved to be baseless, destructive, unfounded, and in many cases downright foolish or decades out of date.

With this chapter, I hope insights into my personal challenges help you explore and establish a baseline for your own concerns or subliminal prejudices. Consider the myths you've been raised with and internalized. Explore in your own mind the opportunities that are out there once you conquer these myths and dismiss them. From Europe to the Americas to Africa, the Middle East, Asia or somewhere in between—the reality is almost never what we've been led to expect.

When we stoke our fears and biases by consuming and perpetuating these myths, we risk engaging in self-fulfilling prophecy at worst or missed and delayed opportunities at best. I absolutely loved my time in Asia—so much so that after avoiding the region for years, I've returned three times in the past two years.

Fear is part of what makes travel rewarding, but, only when we acknowledge and face it in a way that lets us learn from it. Building towards that mastery can also be crippling, particularly when we wait to face it. Time and time again, what travel teaches us is an important life lesson—the things and outcomes we fear are often far worse in our heads than in reality. The truth of the moment is much more often rewarding, educational and far from traumatic. It is something that enriches us as individuals.

Racism

When I first penned a blog post on the racial realizations outlined in this chapter, I was concerned about how it would be received. Writing on race is a surefire way to piss off just about everyone, not to mention if I fail to accurately convey the heart of my message in just the right way, I stand a good chance at coming across as a complete asshole. Still, I think it's worth including here because I think the realizations, fears, and issues that I'll run through in this chapter are very real and the issues are ones that many of you may also secretly share and be curious about.

There's a very famous quote, generally attributed to Mark Twain that states, "Travel is fatal to prejudice, bigotry, and narrow-mindedness, and many of our people need it sorely on these accounts. Broad, wholesome, charitable views of men and things cannot be acquired by vegetating in one little corner of the earth all one's lifetime."

Travel long enough and you'll run into this quote, often in abbreviated form, found plastered across guide books, blogs, and articles dedicated to travel. It embodies the beauty of travel. It also conveys some of the power of travel.

As a veteran traveler, a lot of my prejudices and biases were eroded away a long time ago. I was lucky enough to grow up in a household that focused heavily on education while striving to teach a message of respect, inclusion, and evaluation based on individual merits—not race or ethnic origin.

Still, as I prepared for my first visit to Sub-Saharan Africa—a continent I had never before set foot upon or, to be candid, had a strong desire to visit—I was nervous and forced to admit privately, if not publicly, that I was unsure of what to expect.

I had a number of what I knew to be childish fears about simple things…dealing with my lactose intolerance, accepting local's hospitality, squat toilets, a light case of hypochondria and underneath it all, a decent chunk of racially-oriented anxiety. Current events across Europe and the U.S. right now make it clear that race is as important a subject as ever, so, it's something that we, as individuals, have to at least seek to better understand.

One note: I refer to Africans in a general sense throughout this section. This is done to keep things brief despite the issues with such usage stemming from the common but erroneous tendency to assume some sort of homogeneous entity or identity throughout Africa. I fully realize that Africa is incredibly diverse and that it is truly massive with vastly different cultural groups populating each nation. For this chapter, I'm largely focusing on Sub-Saharan Africa and more specifically my experiences in Zambia. However, because I think that similarly powerful experiences and realizations can be had across the majority of Africa's Sub-Saharan countries and because you, as my readers, are more likely to visit a wide range of countries across Africa, I don't want to limit this chapter explicitly to Zambia, Tanzania, and Botswana where I have traveled.

Racial Concerns

It will probably come as no surprise to most of you that the majority of Zambia's population is black—while I didn't find much in the way of concrete data, it looks like about five percent of the population is non-black while the remaining ninety-five percent come from traditional black African ethnic groups. That is, in many ways, the exact opposite of the areas where I grew up and currently live.

Exposed to travel at an early age and being very scientifically minded I've never considered myself to be someone possessed of racial bias. Instead, I understand 'race' as a social category with varied meanings depending on the context. I know the science behind pigmentation, the evolution of our species and how it shaped our outward appearance and the amount of time and differentiation that it took for our ancestors to adapt to different latitudes. Also, at a certain level, I just don't give a damn what someone's racial background is, though I am always fascinated by their cultural background and the identity that has played into making them who they are as well as the rich traditions that go with it.

Still, our appearance does play a role in how we are perceived by others. Attractiveness, height, hair color and ethnicity are all often easily identifiable visual markers that can sway us as we make snap judgments and seek to socially assign people to different groups and categories based on our own cultural assumptions. To this end, race is still a factor that shapes our interactions and our lives. Not just between black and white, but white and Asian, Indian and black, etc.

What is equally interesting from a sociological and travel perspective is when members who regularly occupy a majority position in one region relocate to another where they are suddenly in the minority. This has happened to friends who have moved from Arizona to Japan or India, and it definitely occurred for me when visiting Africa.

Hopefully, you've got friends from different ethnic backgrounds and at some point, you've had an honest conversation with them about the cultural dynamics of your local community. While these conversations may discuss more visible issues like racism, they can also cover other topics like differences in familial or cultural expectations, regional cultural norms, and related topics.

Personally, I've always found these conversations informative and enlightening. Given that the majority of my travel in the lead up to my trip to Zambia and Botswana had been confined to North

America, Europe, Central America and South America, (the trip to Africa pre-dated my visit to Asia), this trip was my first opportunity to really dive headlong into being an easily identified/absolute minority.

Frankly, that made it pretty scary. Especially in light of the stories I've heard from other travelers, volunteers, and expats. After all, for all the racial issues the United States has between whites and blacks, Zambia has many similar challenges...only roles are reversed. I had heard from friends that I'd be targeted by beggars and for bribes from corrupt officials alike, that there would be an added assumption that because I was white, I'd have money and that there were some legitimate safety concerns that I'd need to take into account strictly because of my skin color.

Beyond that though, and perhaps even more disturbing on a personal level, was the realization that while I did not feel like I held an overt racial bias, I did draw on cultural distinctions which generally fell along racial lines. More specifically, while I didn't have a racial bias against minorities in situations where I was a member of the majority, the thought of being a minority among what still registered internally as a very different racial majority made me somewhat uncomfortable.

I think this can be traced in large part back to an inherent racial bias which is still ingrained in American culture at a deep level with ties back to segregation and slavery. This semi-emotional response flew in the face of what I know at a cognitive level—that people are people, cultures are cultures, and that physical differences in skin tone are every bit as irrelevant as eye color.

Yet I found myself annoyed by my own internal automatic response and wondering if I wasn't just buying my own version of feel-good bullshit. All the while embracing the age-old pat yourself on the back racism that pretends that just because you've got a black friend, you can't have racial biases or be racist. The end result was that as I prepared to leave, I found myself wondering just how many of the racial myths and biases that I thought I had overcome, I had never completely outgrown.

What Zambia and Botswana Taught Me

Boom, wheels down in Zambia and a rapid fast forward into the first week of my visit. It was a year after my brother had first deployed with the U.S. Peace Corps as a health volunteer to a remote village in Zambia, where he'd go on to serve the full duration of his two-year service. Still adjusting and freshly arrived from Denmark, I found myself in the northwestern part of Zambia on the outskirts of a village of about 1,000 people sitting on the stoop of my brother's hut which lacked electricity or running water.

To say we were a bit off the beaten tourist path would have been a reasonable understatement. My parents and I were very likely the third, fourth, and fifth white people many of the local village kids had ever seen. My brother and another nearby Peace Corps volunteer being the other two. We were unusual. We were different. We were a curiosity, and for the sake of this chapter, we were most definitely a minority.

Culture shock was pervasive and never-ending: The kids would stand for as long as an hour at the end of the path to my brother's hut just watching us as we went about our daily business. It was an odd experience, and henceforth I'll forever have an added bit of sympathy for celebrities facing off with the paparazzi and even more so for minorities who similarly are singled out every day as the outside 'other'.

Later, when joining my brother's Zambian counterparts for a meal or conversation, the local kids would pause their football games to stand nervously watching us. Eventually, if we approached them, they'd shyly introduce themselves unsure just what to make of us. With the older kids and adults, the invisible wall was different, more thickly disguised, but still present.

Now that I've returned to Denmark and had the time to digest my experience, I've come to realize that one of the best parts of the trip was the time I spent as an absolute minority. Not because I liked it, or I particularly cared for the differences in how I was treated, but rather because it gave me the opportunity to be truly immersed and exposed to almost entirely black communities.

As I reflect on my relationships with friends, many of whom come from minority backgrounds and some of whom are a mixture of both black and African Americans, I've come to realize that my relationships with these individuals are wonderful but don't have the extended scope I would have previously thought. In reality, the friendships have done little to break down my own personal version of the African school children's exotic uncertainty. Until Africa, I had never had the chance to be truly immersed in a black community that showcased individuals of all trades, social classes, and ages. My interactions before the trip had largely fallen within the extremes: Most of them were either with blacks and African Americans who were well-educated, motivated, driven individuals like myself, and who were usually around my age, or individuals and experiences at the opposite end of the spectrum.

That type of contrast makes it almost impossible to truly understand and relate to a group—no matter what type of group it is. It also polarizes the nature of our interactions. It is interesting and to our own detriment that we often pretend that this isn't the case. Which isn't to assume that everyone reading this is a white American from a heavily Caucasian community—I know all of you come from vastly different experiences. But, hopefully, you'll be able to draw parallels within your own life and community.

Most importantly, what I found so completely powerful and persuasive about my time in Zambia and Botswana was that it allowed me to truly immerse myself in a way that was lethal to those stereotypes. It exposed me to wonderful people of all ages, professions, backgrounds, and ideologies in a way that fully rounded out my previously limited experiences. The sheer contrast was a key part of this, and helped differentiate it from my time spent in Belize which also has a large black population but lacked the extreme contrast and immersion that made my time in Zambia so meaningful.

I'm not sure if this was because I spent more time confined to the tourist trail while in Belize, my general expectations, a combination of the two, or some other factor but the end result was a drastically different experience. Perhaps it was actually more basic than that, and had more to do with my own attentiveness and the lens I observed the world through.

Regardless, while I don't think that I entered Africa with a pronounced case of, as Twain put it, "prejudice, bigotry, and narrow-mindedness", I know that by the time I left Africa what ghosts of these traits I may have still possessed had been brought out into the open and largely banished. Where they still persist, like cobwebs in rafters of a room, I now acknowledge and am aware of their existence.

The real beauty of the learning process and what came with it is that it simultaneously opened up a new area of exploration and discovery—one that focuses on Euro-American-African relations, history, and the issues of race and culture that go with it. By re-examining my own subconscious behaviors and dismantling some of the most subliminal, I'm also able to enjoy richer interactions which shape everything from the people I befriend to the women I seriously consider as potential romantic partners.

You're a Minority Somewhere

I can still remember vividly the first time my brother, who had by that point spent more than a year in Zambia with the U.S. Peace Corps as a health volunteer, firmly corrected my use of 'reverse racism' in conversations. I don't recall the specifics, but it had something to do with some of the challenges that arose from being a minority. "Reverse racism," he asked, "what's that?" As I started to clarify and elaborate a bit, surprised by his confusion, he cut me off. "Racism is racism."

Ultimately, we're all members of complex social and racial groups. Racism isn't a white vs. black or black vs. Hispanic or Asian vs. white dynamic. Racism is simple in its flexibility and that, as much as anything, is also something that is essential to remember.

My goal in sharing these musings and observations with you is to help encourage you to be honest with yourself, to be honest about your motivations, about your preconceptions and what they mean for you as you go to organize and plan a potential trip. Keep in mind that while these experiences and realizations reflect my personal insights as I explored Zambia, you may find similar ones as you venture into different cultural regions. It is also worth noting that in many ways the essence of these same realizations may hold true for Zambians making their first trip to the United States or Europe.

The final key consideration tied to race and related issues, which I hope you'll consider, is the emerging concept of self-licensing/moral-licensing. Earlier in this chapter I mentioned the age-old defense often used to justify bad behavior where one references their black, or gay, or female or jewish or . . . friend as evidence that they're not actually racist /sexist/bigoted. Self-licensing highlights the behavior that we're all guilty of to some degree or another. It highlights situations where we take one basic and limited action, then use that action as currency in the bank to justify and license future behaviors that are contradictory.

In this way the bigot can point to President Obama's ascention to the presidency and use that as license to justify and rebuke any racially descriminatory or limiting behavior moving forward. In Malcom Gladwell's podcast *Revisionist History's* "The Lady Vanishes," he introduces the concept of moral/self-licensing from the perspective of women's rights. His examples include *The Roll Call* by Elizabeth Thompson, a powerful and ground breaking painting by a woman as well as the election of Australia's first female Prime Minister, Julia Gillard. Both vividly highlight just how damaging moral licensing can be.

It's effectively the ethical equivelent of taking a tiny flight of stairs instead of the escalator in the metro on your way home from the metro. Actually, scratch that. Not even a flight of stairs. More like walking the two steps to bypass the ramp to the elevator. Then using that as justification that you've been healthy, worked out and earned the right to eat an entire tub of ice cream. In terms of racial bias, simply having that one black friend does not suddenly give you license to abandon your self work on breaking down racial barriers and bias or mean that you're free of them.

Regardless of where you are in the journey, I hope you'll embrace the challenge, welcome it, and push yourself to connect with people. To reach out to them. To understand them. To learn from them and eventually to allow whatever deeply buried prejudice, bigotry, or well-intentioned ignorance you may harbor to be burned away by the experience. My time in Africa not only offered rich experiences and improved my internal person, but it left me prepared to be a better brother to my fellow human beings.

Picking Travel Partners

You're itching to take a trip. You've got the money saved up, or at least you are ready to start saving for it, have a general idea where you really want to go, when you can go and are almost all set. Yet, you're stuck. You're missing one of the key pieces of the equation—someone to travel with.

While I'm a huge advocate of solo-travel and I constantly encourage people to try it, the truth is there are a lot of destinations which are best seen with company. Unfortunately, while travel is almost always a pleasant experience, traveling with other people tends to have a significantly higher failure rate. Beyond ruining the experience, it also has an unfortunate tendency to scrap friendships and relationships in the process.

All of which sounds a bit dire. But, the good news is that when it does work out, it has the potential to cement friendships and craft them into lifelong relationships. Traveling together also creates a string of new shared memories which adds an incredible level of depth and richness above and beyond simply navigating life's daily routines together.

In general, most people get so caught up in feeling

that they have to find a travel companion or feeling obliged to travel with a close friend or someone who they're unsure about, that they neglect basic best practice from the get-go.

You're going to live together for the duration of the trip, hang out together, eat together and be in a plethora of emotionally-charged situations. Chances are, the trip will also stretch across days, not just a sunny afternoon or cozy morning.

The following are key elements I use to evaluate a travel partner (or partners) compatibility.

Travel Experience

As a casual weekend hiker would you enter an Ironman contest with a veteran Ironman contestant? Probably not. Why? Because your goals, experience, conditioning, and approach are fundamentally different. This is an important lesson when picking a travel partner. While not an exact science, travelers can be broken down into three easy categories: novice, intermediate and expert travelers.

When trying to find a travel partner it initially appears to make sense that novice travelers should seek out expert travelers as companions. It's like having a guide, but better—right? Not really, and in most cases, it's a bad idea for a fairly simple reason: Expert travelers tend to be at a very different place with their desired experiences, where they find value, and their travel goals.

Travel for a novice traveler is flush with brand new experiences, even on the most basic levels. These are the things that make travel terrifying but also add fantastic depth to it. The novice traveler is far more inclined to want to see every museum, every major historic landmark, and to stop at major tourist destinations. For most, they're at a stage that mirrors a child's love and lust for discovery, and that should be embraced and nurtured. And, just to be completely clear—yeah, that means photographing the first twenty cobblestone streets you see and posing for every cliché tourist photo you feel tempted to pose for along the way. All without guilt or apology.

The challenge comes when you try and pair a traveler in that novice state with someone who has already gone through that phase. They've not only seen many of the major cathedrals and architectural wonders but have probably done tens if not hundreds of museums… and if they've spent time in Europe this likely includes the main museums in England, France, Italy and Greece which house the lion's share of the world's most famous wonders.

For many of these experienced travelers, the experience has shifted from observation to immersion. They're still setting a fast pace at times but their approach is usually more haphazard, and they may not go out of their way to chase pure novelty experiences. They also typically travel slower, are on tighter budgets, and relate very differently to their environment.

As far as the intermediate traveler? They're ordinarily a combination of the two—somewhere in the middle as they transition from wide-eyed novice to storied veteran. It's also not always cut and dried. Depending on the region and culture or travel style, we tend to fluctuate, which is another dimension to bear in mind. Just because your companion has back-packed the world for a year, don't necessarily assume that they're well versed on the logistics and experiences of luxury spa-based travel.

Travel Style

While similar to the topic of Travel Experience, travel style is an essential factor when planning a trip. It's important to keep in mind that travel style varies depending on country/destination and tends to evolve over time. Take a few minutes to sit down and really think about what your travel style is (or might be).

Do you enjoy well-organized trips or spontaneous wandering? Do you prefer to be active in the mornings or the afternoons? Camping, homestays, hostels, hotels or resorts? What is more important to you, an afternoon spent exploring a niche museum or one spent sitting at a small cafe reading a book? These questions have a tendency to help you narrow in on specific answers that can make a huge difference.

Budget

Money. It ruins friendships, marriages, and can make or break a trip. For most of us, travel is a leisure expense. Something we have to save up for, which is optional, and tends to be an increase over our day-to-day budget. Beyond that though, most of us have widely varied spending habits.

Figuring out your budget and what classifies as an acceptable quality of life while on the road is an essential part of trip preparation. Far less talked about, however, is the importance of making sure your budget and financial means line up with those of the person you're looking to travel with.

They seldom do.

Which is why setting a budget, which you both intend to stick to, is essential. What happens if you miss a train or get stuck paying twice what you budgeted for a hotel room? While it may be within what you can afford, can your travel partner? Or, how do you plan to divide up your expenses? If you and your travel partner have both budgeted $100/day, you've agreed to the preliminary threshold, but that doesn't mean you're done. As the old adage goes, the devil really is in the details. How much of that will go to accommodation, food, beer and/or entertainment costs?

Do your budgets and values coincide? If they do, then a trip is a safe bet. If they don't, you're probably better off finding a more suitable group or individual to travel with.

Fresh Air

Agree before the trip starts to spend some time apart. Far too often when scheduling a trip, sometimes even trips that will last months, it's not uncommon to spend nearly every waking (and dreaming) moment together. As time passes that becomes more and more of a challenge even for the best of friends (or couples) and let's face it, your travel partner may be great, but there's no guarantee they're your best friend.

Before you leave, have a conversation about working in free days where you both split up and spend the day doing your own thing. I'd suggest working in one every week and a half or so, but it will depend widely on how well you travel together. What's important is that you recognize when you need space and are able to take it without any hurt feelings.

Even though my brother and I travel incredibly well together and have the added advantage of being able to tell each other off when something is annoying, we still benefit from and periodically take solo-afternoons. Far too often people tend to feel that to do so is some sort of expectation of failure—a veritable traveler's pre-nup that dooms the undertaking to failure. Which is, of course, bullshit.

Timing and Commitment

Two rules tend to shape the lead-up to a trip. People are flaky, and life happens. You've planned a trip, started saving, found a travel partner, and then a month before the trip, you learn they either haven't saved up the money they planned to, have made other plans, or chickened out. Now you're without a travel partner, the prices of airfare have gone up, and you're left high and dry. Trip ruined, all before it even began.

My advice is to let actions speak louder than words. Don't let your desperation to find a travel partner or eagerness to travel with someone cripple or kill your trip. Set firm deadlines for ticket purchases and get your potential travel partner financially invested as quickly as possible. The easiest way to make a trip "real" is to purchase your airline tickets. While this isn't 100 percent, it will improve the follow-through rate and weed out people who love the idea and are saying yes but would otherwise flake out later down the road.

If they can't or won't commit within a reasonable time period, it's time to move on and find someone else. At the end of the day, it's ok to be a bit selfish. This is your trip, and you're responsible for making it happen. Set yourself up to succeed, not fail.

Numbers Games

Remember the old saying, *the more the merrier?* When it comes to travel, it's bullshit. The larger the group, the more difficult and frustrating the trip will be. That's a simple fact. As a general rule of thumb more than three people should never travel together for more than a week (unless part of an organized tour). Remember that even adding one person triples all of the factors outlined in this section.

Are there groups that do it with more? You bet. Did they survive the trip in one piece and as one group? Sometimes. Did any make it through without significant frustration at some point or another? Probably not. Also, don't underestimate the added complexities that come with larger groups from the emergence of multiple aspiring leaders to inter-group dating and sexual drama. There's also the often significant loss of time and increased energy dedicated to daily activity planning as you work to align to everyone's desires.

You Have Two Months to Define the Experience

I remember the surreal exhilaration as I took that first step onto Danish soil. Even as a veteran traveler I still couldn't help but feel a bit like Neil Armstrong as he stepped out from the lunar lander into the unknown. For me, it was the start of a two-year full degree program at the University of Copenhagen and a radical change from my lifestyle over the previous three years spent working nine to five in the mergers and acquisitions industry.

I was incredibly excited but also positively terrified. At the time it was all a bit overwhelming but, as I look back, it was one of the best experiences of my life. It was a major learning lesson where I made missteps and could have done some things better. Overall though, I made a lot of great decisions and have relatively few regrets. Every bit as significant, I learned something very important about how we live our lives and how rapidly we adapt to new opportunities.

Over the past few years, I've worked with a lot of international students and expats who have been engaged in a variety of different programs which range from semester exchanges and multi-year full degree programs to expat relocations. In so doing I've noticed a couple of trends which are deeply ingrained in human behavior which can do a lot to shape how much a person gets out of their international experience. Chief among these is tied to their behavior during the early-arrival period and how they form their daily routines.

These lessons are most easily recognized and relevant in the beginning, but the lesson can be applied to any time we uproot from one heavily entrenched and established environment and find ourselves transplanted into a completely new one.

Simply put, if you want to get a lot out of the experience, there are a few basic things you have to do during the stage immediately after you start/ arrive. This period of flexibility and opportunity is fleeting and lasts somewhere in the neighborhood of a couple of weeks to—at most—two months. How long depends a lot on personal adaptability and connections to the familiar. The individuals that really dive in and make themselves take action have an experience with few regrets and a much richer sense of fulfillment than those who don't.

Even the most spontaneous of us is still a creature of habit. Some studies have shown that our daily activities can be predicted with ninety-three percent certainty and that we typically don't travel beyond a six-mile radius except on special occasions. These routines are very rarely disrupted, but when they are, it usually doesn't take long for us to replace them with new ones.

The opportunity to relocate from one country to another is one of the most extreme and unusual breaks in our daily routine we'll ever experience. This is part of what makes the experience so scary but, it is also an incredible opportunity, particularly if we go into it aware that within a relatively short period of time we'll have re-established our new routine and be back on a normal schedule.

One of the biggest regrets from students at the

end of their study abroad period is that they didn't see and do more. Almost without fail they express disbelief that they didn't make it to key sites, discover favorite locations, or participate fully in a lot of rewarding activities until the very end of their experience when things were rushed and the impending weight of their return home inescapable. While this is almost unavoidable, that departure remorse is much worse for people who failed to push themselves during their first two months.

Why? Because upon arrival, there is a sense of being overwhelmed. After all, it is stressful and exhausting to make new friends, learn a new culture, explore a new city, and attempt to satisfy academic or professional requirements at the same time. It's very easy during this period to seek out things that are familiar and comfortable. For many, the belief is that they'll spend the first month or two getting established and building a safe nest, and then, once they've built that comfortable base, they'll set out to explore the city, its events, and venues more completely.

Unfortunately, at that point, it almost never happens and is often too late. Once established, that comfortable routine is very difficult to break free of in any significant way. Not because you won't want to or know you need to, but excuses will always come up, and the day-to-day needs of a regular lifestyle will become all consuming.

As hard as it is, this means that even when exhausted, when feeling homesick, and even if alone and as-yet still friendless, during that first two-month period it's important to spend every moment and every opportunity trying new things and new places.

If you or someone you know is about to engage in a dramatic lifestyle change or relocation, make a deal with yourself—for every time you visit a coffee shop or eat a meal at a place you've been to before, find and visit two new places.

Thinking you'll wait until visitors come to visit the tourist stuff around the city? Don't. It has a habit of not happening, and when visitors arrive, you'll take them to places you know, not places you haven't been to. Force yourself to explore, to wander, and to visit the tourist sites and attractions in your first couple of weeks because after that two-month mark hits you will start to form habits and settle in.

Which is fine. One of the best parts of living abroad is the feeling of truly being settled in and starting to integrate into where you live. *But*, if you haven't done your research and haven't explored and experienced a wide selection of what's available before settling into that routine you've effectively gone to a large buffet for lunch, tried the first food that was conveniently available from the buffet, decided it tasted reasonably good, and then eaten that exclusively for the remainder of your meal.

If you follow this advice and hit the ground running while really pushing yourself to get out there, you're going to have a better feel for the city. You're also going to meet more people, be exposed to more events, and have much better opportunities than an individual who doesn't. It is a simple thing, but it is also one of the things you can do that will radically improve your experience.

This is equally relevant for building your social

group and identity. Keep in mind that we are always influenced by the people we surround ourselves with. They inspire us. They challenge us and they shape our habits and behaviors. Early on the temptation is to grasp for anyone who is similarly available. The risk, however, is that these individuals will form the basis for your freshly minted social network moving forward and will have a profound impact on the new routines and identity that emerge as you form habits.

Of course, what's happening at an underlying level can be equally relevant to major life changes such as a divorce or breakup that forces a revisiting of your social network.

As a result, I cannot stress enough how important being aware of these breaks in our long-established routines can be. When you find yourself in or seek out and create one of these opportunities, the clock starts ticking immediately.

Enjoy and embrace the uncertainty, make it your own, discover it, and tackle it head on. You'll never forgive yourself if you don't. I just wish I was in your shoes and could do it all again. Not because I'm not happy with how I did it but, because in retrospect, that rush, that sense of discovery, that conquest of the unknown, and that control over reshaping my daily life was an incredible transformative experience.

THE ROADS WILL OPEN
UP FOR YOU

As you turn these final pages, I hope that I have provided you with fuel to ignite new areas for personal investigation and reflection. Though much of our lives and the way we are educated attempts to limit topics to a specific genre or focus area, I hope *Practical Curiosity* has helped alter or enhance your relationship with cross-disciplinary knowledge and its value.

I have always aspired to the ideal of being a Renaissance man and polymath; to nurture a burning curiosity across disciplines, with each informing and enhancing my understanding of the other. Yet, this has brought with it, as I believe is often the case, quite a few challenges, a fair bit of discomfort, and uncertainty. Yet, the ultimate outcome is the ability to see and engage with the world in a far more vibrant and multi-dimensional way.

With *Practical Curiosity* I set out to share the pivotal observations and realizations that I find most formative or which are part of the silent (and not so silent) reoccurring struggles in the lives of friends, colleagues, travelers, and peers. Now, with the sum of these pages read, as the process of digesting begins, I hope that you'll reflect on each individual section and how it resonated with you. At the same time, try and take a fresh look at yourself, your habits, fears, and behaviors informed and contextualized by the observations, thought exercises, and ways of reflecting highlighted throughout this book. As you do you will break down barriers that are limiting your growth and success.

A life defined and shaped by curiosity is a life guaranteed to be infused with richness, even though that can come at a cost. Ultimately, it is a more challenging path than the alternative and that is something that we don't acknowledge as much as we should. For a balanced and healthy life it is important to be practical, realistic, and kind to ourselves as we nurture our inherent curiosity. For those driven by a particularly strong sense of curiosity, take heart, what strike you as abnormalities are just reflections of a way of thinking and a profile that varies from the status quo.

I hope that you'll use advocacy, compassionate listening, and more ethical ways of relating as you live, love and travel to teach, educate and internalize your own lessons.

I also hope that this book has helped you better understand and accept yourself, your decisions, and the life path you've chosen and will chart for yourself moving forward. Above all else, don't forget to step back and to accept that you are on a learner's journey. The beauty of tomorrow is that it provides us with new opportunities to experiment, to explore, and to craft ourselves into who and what we want to become, letting go of the parts of ourselves that we have outgrown.

This book is intended as a starting point. Each section is written to serve as little more than a preface and casual introduction to topics which are much deeper and often include wonderful and at times vexing nuances and contradictions. So, dog-ear or highlight the sections that most catch your interest and then dive into an investigation of your own.

Thank you for choosing to fuel your curiosity with this book. Thank you to all those who have and will continue to inspire. Looking forward, the roads will open up for you. Great adventures and wonderful discoveries are just ahead.

ABOUT THE AUTHOR

Alex is a profoundly curious person with a passion for communication, entrepreneurship, governance, and human behavior. That curiosity has led him to tickle a wild polar bear's nose, found him stranded on a grounded ferry in the no-man's-land between Belize and Mexico, and taken him to more than fifty countries.

With degrees in human Cognition and Communication, Alex has long dabbled in entrepreneurialism with a specialization in innovative approaches to digital communities. He has found career success in the commercial real estate, mergers and acquisitions, bio technology, and advertising technology industries. In addition he is a globally recognized blogger, podcaster, photographer, and videographer. Alex also enjoys delivering public talks and guest lectures.

Alex has been traveling since before he could walk. His wanderlust was cemented at the age of eleven when the family rented their house, packed a year's worth of possessions into four backpacks, and caught a plane to Europe. Two years later the family struck out once again for a year of travel across the United States in a thirty-two-foot fifth-wheel trailer.

Since relocating in 2011, Alex has lived and worked in Copenhagen, Denmark.

Continue the conversation at
practicalcuriosity.com

57245173R00117

Made in the USA
Middletown, DE
16 December 2017